LARS WESTERLUND

The Extended Arm of Man

A History of the Industrial Robot

INFORMATIONSFÖRLAGET

Illustrations
ABB FRONT COVER, S. 3, 24, 33, 43, 45, 49, 50,
52, 53, 55, 57, 59, 60, 61, 65, 74, 89, 90, 91, 100,
101, 122, 123, 124, 127, 128, 130, 131, 132, 135,
139, 143, 145, 148, 155, 158, 159, 161, 164, 167.
BUSINESS WEEK 96. COMAU 81. ELECTROLUX 37.
FOTOGRAF ROLF PETTERSSON 35. GENERAL
ELECTRIC 28. HELPMATE 20,163. HE MASKIN-
SERVICE 38. IBL BILDBYRÅ 16, 20, 64, 69, 77, 86,
92, 95, 97, 98, 107, 110, 113, 117. KOCKUMS 40.
KUKA 161. NEOS ROBOTICS 151. PRESSENS BILD
117. SVERIGES TEKNISKA ATTACHÉER 78, 97,
106, 108. SWIRA 68, 71, 75, 97, 119, 156. TEK-
NISKA MUSEET, STOCKHOLM 11, 13.

This book has also been published in Swedish with the title
Människans förlängda arm. En bok om industrirobotens historia.
Translation: Paul Bray and Carl Kerns, Skellefteå.

© 2000 Informationsförlaget and the author
Author: Lars Westerlund, Westerlunds Reportagebyrå, Skellefteå
Project leaders: ABB Robotics: Christina Bredin and Sven Sjöqvist
Art editor: Catarina Sundberg, Westerlunds Reportagebyrå
Graphic design: Ulf Lindahl, Stockholm
Production manager: Bokform Majbritt Hagdahl. Stockholm
Printed in 2000 by Centraltryckeriet, Borås
ISBN 91-7736-467-8

Informationsförlaget, Box 6884, 113 86 Stockholm
Telephone 08-34 09 15, fax 08-31 39 03
E-mail red@informationsforlaget.se
www.informationsforlaget.se

FOREWORD

THIS BOOK TELLS THE STORY behind the development of the industrial robot, focusing on the events of the past 25 years – a long time in terms of today's IT product development but still a relatively short time for establishing a completely new range of products in the world market. Personally, I regard these 25 years of development as both fast and slow.

Fast with regard to the rate of growth in numbers and maturity, especially in the automotive industry around the world. It is almost unheard of today to hand-weld a car body and the naked robot, after 25 years, is now considered a mature product.

Nevertheless, slow in advancing the boundaries of applications and user industries. While the number of robots in the automotive industry has grown at a record rate, their expansion into other industries and service areas has been very slow.

This combination has brought us to the situation where industrial robots have become a large world-spanning industry that is considered mature by many yet still with most of their potential ahead of us, both in technical development and their establishment.

THE DEVELOPMENT OF ABB robots started 25 years ago and it must be said that Asea was a good base from which to start. It was a heavy and traditional company, certainly, but with superb expertise within key areas such as electric power and control, mechanical design and even production technique. In addition, they had a leader like the Swede, Curt Nicolin, whose technical background gave him a clear sight of the opportunity for business development and was prepared to press on.

The robot project received much attention during its initial stages in 1972–74. There was strong pressure from above, handpicked key players to form a group and a clear mandate to act independently. The robot design was an unknown quantity. The result was an electric robot with one of Sweden's first microprocessor control systems. The challenge was to present a prototype for the Asea board, headed by Swedish industrialist Marcus Wallenberg, after just ten months.

THESE WERE THE EARLY BEGINNINGS. The continued development, which is described in this book, progressed in several stages:

– First, the project, through which it was imperative to establish a working, selling and trendsetting concept for the robot as a product in the European market. This was the main emphasis in the seventies.

– Then, market development, through which it was imperative to establish the new electric robot concept in the global market; Europe and even USA and Japan together with the rest of Asia. This took place largely during the eighties.

– Subsequently, system development with functional packages to offer the customer a system that is both standardised and customised. The ambition was there all the time but most of the development took place during the nineties.

– Finally, and perhaps most importantly, continuous business development to rationalise and develop competitiveness in an aggressive global market that up to now had demanded improved performance and large price-cuts every year. This pressure will only become more intense.

THE PROGRESS HAS HAD ITS CRITICAL points, of course. Certain system projects have been a loss, certain robot markets have been discontinued and profits were strained by entering new markets during the eighties. However, the management at ABB has always given their support to this vast project.

It gives me great pleasure now to see that the project has become a profitable multi-million industry and that the ABB robot operations at the turn of the millennium are world-leaders after 25 years' work; in a market that has installed over one million robots! And it will continue to grow. These 25 years have really become part of industrial history!

On the eve of the 21st century, I can see the robot industry well prepared for further progress in terms of volume, at least in the immediate future. These will be born by the products of today and those presently under development. As yet, we have only covered a small portion of the needs of the mechanical industry for flexible automation.

In the long term, however, I believe that the robot industry must expand its horizons and present new ideas for user industries, including the service sector, which is also demanding new technology. Eventually, when sensors and man-machine communication has been further developed, there will be an enormous potential market for personal robots.

Irrespective of the direction that development takes, I believe ABB Robotics is well equipped with expertise, market knowledge and strong personnel resources. I am proud to have been part of the first 18 years and wish you luck in the future.

I would also like to take this opportunity to thank everybody that has contributed to this book.

Björn Weichbrodt
Federation of Swedish Manufacturing Industries
Sveriges Verkstadsindustrier
ABB Robotics 1971–89

CONTENTS

I | The Past History of Industrial Robots

WHERE DID THE FIRST THOUGHTS concerning industrial robots emerge?

Ask that question and you will probably receive different answers from anyone given the chance to express their opinion. However, the story of the industrial robot, which has only taken its first stumbling steps on an increasingly competitive market as we approach the twenty-first century, must begin somewhere.

Some industrial historians would probably go all the way back to the playful engineer Heron from Alexandria who lived in the 1st century BC to find the roots of industrial robots. Anyway, he was before his time when it came to automation. Among other things, he invented an impressive system that automatically opened the doors to the most holy of rooms in the temple by using the energy created when the altar fire was lit. Heron also constructed water-driven songbirds and an "aeolipile", a device used to transform steam into rotary motion.

Early Swedish impulses

Being Swedish, it comes naturally to give some of the credit to the innovator and entrepreneur Christoffer Polhem. During a journey in France and England, Polhem saw how the manufacture of metal and textile was changing. Hydropower and wind power were being used more often when hand tools were replaced by automatic tools. Polhem realised that Sweden, given its resources of power, could benefit greatly from such techno-

CHAPTER 1

The past history of industrial robots

logy. At Stjernsund's works, built in 1700, he constructed machines to cut out cogwheels for clocks using hydropower. Among other things, he developed an early form of milling machine. Until then, each individual clockmaker had filed his own cogwheels by hand, which was time consuming work that demanded precision. When Polhem came with ready-made sets of cogwheels, the clockmakers were at first reluctant to buy them. Producing everything by hand was a matter of professional pride.

Polhem was responsible for many constructions that rationalised manual work; spinning machines for the textile industry and rolling mills for sheet metal that was then made into mugs, plates and cutlery in Stjernsund's various hammer shops. Metal objects for civil use had never before been mass-produced. Automation led to the work being divided into stages, each one as simple as possible to carry out.

That machines took over heavy and time consuming manual work is something we take for granted today but, at that time, it was ingenious.

Decrease in child labour and violent protests

At the end of the 17th century, child labour was very common in the fast-growing textile industries. One of the people this made indignant was Frenchman Joseph Marie Jacquard. In the silk mill where he worked, children sat on top of the weaving looms operating the mechanism. In 1801, Jacquard patented his punch-card loom.

CHAPTER 1
*The past history
of industrial robots*

Despite the fact that machines improved the working environment and contributed to less child labour, there were still people who were against automation in the textile industry. In England, for instance, a resistance movement was started called the Luddites, named after its leader Ned Ludd. In 1811 the protests increased even more.

The birth of the computer industry

In 1886, American Herman Hollerith introduced a machine that would mean a great deal to automation and later to robotics. It was a punch card machine used for population censuses. The cards were passed over a metal surface where wire brushes pierced through the holes, made contact and closed electric circuits. The machine could be programmed to search for different data, such as profession or number of children. Each card that gave a certain answer could be sorted automatically, electrically, into a box.

When USA carried out the population census of 1890, it was the first time the results were not counted by hand. Hollerith's machine saved years of counting, which would otherwise have rendered the results out of date. Hollerith's pioneering invention laid the foundations for the computer company IBM.

Taylorism and the T-Ford

Fredrick Taylor from the USA was the first to introduce a scientific

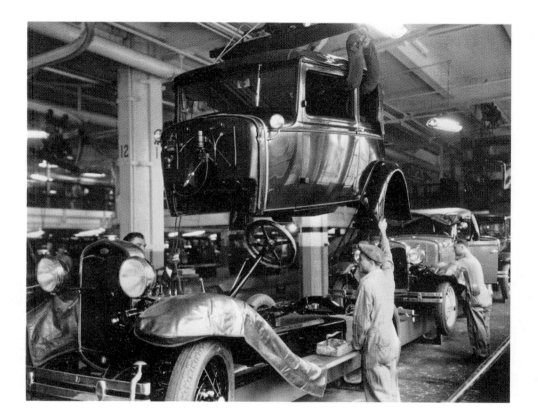

Henry Ford mass-produced the Model T-Ford on an assembly line. He was inspired by Frederick Taylor's ideas on smarter working methods to increase production.

method for structuring work in the factory. According to his theories, which were formed in the 1880s, the workforce should not work harder to increase production but work smarter. Taylor regarded heavy work from a scientific point of view; he studied time expenditure and work methods.

Car manufacturer Henry Ford embraced Taylor's thoughts and then began to mass-produce his T-Ford on assembly lines. Ford helped to cut the cost of factory produced goods, while at the same time improving the working conditions for the factory workers. The car's frame was passed from station to station, to which parts were delivered on a parallel belt. Each worker had only one or two tasks to perform, decreasing the demand for skilled workers.

The assembly line contributed to a reduction in the price of a T-Ford from 850 dollars in 1908 to 260 dollars in 1925. The work, however, was boring and the assembly workers often stayed for only a short time. However, this was to change when the wages rose far above that in other industries.

Powerful computers

The development of computers continued after the Second World War. The first electronic computer used in the civil sector was the ENIAC (Electronic Numerical Integrator and Calculator) constructed by Americans John Mauchly and Presper Eckert at the University of Pennsylvania in 1946. The computer was an enormous contraption, 26 metres long, consisting of 18,000 electronic tubes and weighing over 30 tons. The computer performed 100 times the number of operations per second than a conventional relay based machine could. Among other things, it was used for weather forecasting and wind tunnel testing. This was essentially the start of the modern computer era.

The transistor, invented in 1948 by John Bardeen, Walter Bratton and William Schokley at Bell Labs, was eventually to be used in increasingly smaller and more powerful computers together with integrated circuits. They became the brains in industrial robots in the early seventies.

Originate from NC machines

Technically, you could say that industrial robots originate from hydraulic assembly machines that arrived in the 1950s and from the NC machines (numerically controlled turning and milling machines). The Swedish descendant J. Parson led the development of the first advanced NC machine, which was presented at MIT in Boston 1951.

The arrival of the NC machine was a technical breakthrough. The machine was programmed using only numbers and it could easily be reset for short series. It was now possible to work with more complicated designs.

The automation debate

Del Harder became technical director at Ford in 1946. He wanted to establish a completely automatic production line and launched the concept of automation. Soon, the company had an automation department working on optimising the use of equipment and increasing productivity. Ford's ventures led to a world-wide debate on automation. The critics were of the opinion that automation was designed to rationalise workers out of production and they predicted mass unemployment. On the other hand, there were also strong supporters of automation who were of the opinion that automation would lead to "the second industrial revolution".

There was a strong scepticism at this time towards exceedingly advanced machines. Del himself never applied the word "robot" to the rationalisation process in his enterprise.

The contribution of Charlie Chaplin's film Modern Times, made in 1936, was effective in the debate concerning the automation of factories in the USA.

Rossum's robot

The term robot was actually launched as early as the 1920s. Robot is a word that exists in several Slavonic languages and originally meant heavy monotonous work or slave labour. The word turned up in the Czechoslovakian playwright Karel Capek's play R.U.R. Rossum's Universal Robots. The play is about worker robots that revolt and kill their human master Rossum and all life on Earth. Capek's robots possessed a combination of super human strength and intelligence. The end of the play aptly takes place in the 1960s, which happened to be the decade when robots made their entry into industry. In the eyes of the people, a robot was generally considered something negative and destructive.

Charlie Chaplin's film Modern Times from 1936 was another powerful weapon in the debate. Through this film, he wanted to show the dark side of the highly automated world.

2 | The Cradle of the American Industrial Robot

A SOCIAL SKILL is a concept that is used today to describe the most important quality of a colleague. Lasse Dencik, a professor in social psychology at the University of Roskilde, usually compares the working life of the future with a cocktail party, where the guests mingle and make new contacts.

It was also during a cocktail party in Connecticut 1956 that it was possible to perceive the embryo of the launch of an industrial robot. One of the guests at this important party was the engineer and innovator George Devol. Two years earlier, he had applied for a patent for a machine that he called Programmed Transfer Article. Devol, however, was uncertain as to how the machine could be used. Another guest at the cocktail party was the 31-year-old engineer Joseph Engelberger, who worked in the space industry. He loved science fiction and he had read all Isaac Asimov's books. The ambitious entrepreneur Engelberger fired on all cylinders when Devol told him about his invention. The idea was equally as exciting after he had recovered from his hangover the morning after the party.

Engelberger, who was very well endowed when it came to social skills, complemented Devol's ingenuity and strong patent position in a constructive way. This meeting between the two men resulted in no less than the start of the company Unimation, the development of the Unimate robot and the birth of the industrial robot industry. Devol was granted his long overdue patent in 1961.

Joseph Engelberger is often called "The Father of Robotics". He is still active in the robot industry and nowadays he is involved in service robots.

George Devol applied for a patent for the first industrial robot in 1954. It was accepted by the American patent office in 1961.

CHAPTER 2

The cradle of the american industrial robot

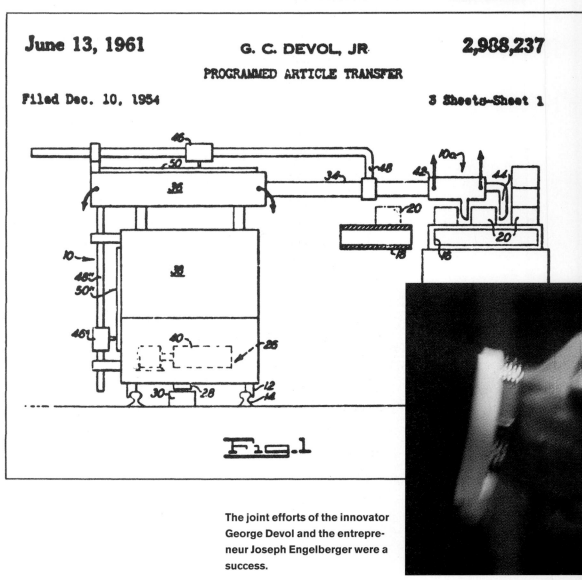

June 13, 1961   G. C. DEVOL, JR.   2,988,237

PROGRAMMED ARTICLE TRANSFER

Filed Dec. 10, 1954   3 Sheets-Sheet 1

Fig.1

The joint efforts of the innovator George Devol and the entrepreneur Joseph Engelberger were a success.

Obtaining capital

Maintaining product development required capital. In 1959, Engelberger succeeded in persuading Norman Schafter at the Consolidated Diesel Engine Company, Condec, to invest money in an industrial robot venture. Engelberger's success in persuasion was not due primarily to the bright future prospects of robot technology but rather to Schafter's burning interest in obtaining expertise for controlling the processes in his factory. Unimation became a subsidiary of Condec.

The Pullman company, who made sleeping coaches for trains, also invested new dollars in robot development; three million to be precise. The money became available when they pulled out of their role as operator on the American railways due to the risk of them ending up in a monopoly position.

The first prototype

Engelberger, Devol and their collaborators visited 15 car factories and around 20 other industries to help them better understand the needs of the industries for industrial robots.

Unimation's hydraulic prototype was completed in 1961 and the first industrial robot was installed to serve a die casting machine in General Motor's factory in Trenton, New Jersey. Compared with the machines of today, it was a fairly simple machine that could only perform one task. The robot cost 65,000 dollars to make but Unimation sold it for 18,000 so it could be used as a reference object. The reason GM was not prepared to pay more was that they wanted a pay-off time of 18 months. Such was the expected life-span.

To increase demand, Unimation initially chose to hire out the machines. This turned out to be a successful move.

Unimation's first industrial robot is now on exhibition at the Smithsonian Institute.

Ford got the manufacturers going

Del Harder at Ford, a man the market listened to when it came to technical development, said on one occasion that he would like to install at least 2,000 robots in his factories. To speed up the industrial robot industry he brazenly copied Unimation's robot specification and sent it to other companies inquiring about the purchase of industrial robots. This inspired a number of large American companies to enter the robotics industry as they now saw the potential of the industrial robot. Among them were AMF, Hughes Aircraft, IBM, Sunstrand and Western Electric.

The Versatran robot

IBM chose early on to sign a licensing agreement with Unimation. They did not talk of industrial robots but instead referred to them as UTD

(Universal Transfer Devices) to avoid the negative connotation that was still associated with the word robot. However, their attempt at twisting words was a total failure; a robot, after all, is always a robot.

In 1958, AMF introduced their Versatran robot, which was to become the biggest threat to the Unimate. A team of engineers, including Harry Johnson, Velijko Milenkovic and Jacob Rabinov, constructed Versatran. In 1962, six Versatran robots were installed in the Ford factory in Canton.

In 1958, Hughes Aircraft produced the first NC machine that could automatically change tools. They even developed robots on behalf of the American Atomic Energy Commission. These robots worked with radioactive material.

The big breakthrough

In 1964, General Motors ordered 66 Unimate robots for their new factory in Lordstown, Ohio. The objective was for this factory to become a model of modern manufacturing techniques. This was an enormous order for Unimation, who had previously built three to four machines a month. One can safely say that this was the big breakthrough for the industrial robot.

The demand for industrial robots was nevertheless still weak and after supplying the order to General Motors, the business returned to its earlier levels of production. However, Engelberger and his partners had been

given proof that industrial robots had a future. They just had to play a waiting game and bide their time until the market was ready.

If the manufacturing industry was not especially quick to adopt robot technology, the media, on the other hand, was all the more interested. Joseph Engelberger and his robots were regular guests on American television. For instance, Unimate robots served coffee on the Johnny Carson show and starred in beer commercials. To the general public, however, the robot was still just a "fun toy".

The first Unimate robot installed
at Ford in the early 60s. It is now
in the Ford museum in Dearborn,
USA.

The first robot to Europe

The first industrial robot was installed in Europe in 1967 when Svenska Metallverken in Upplands Väsby, Sweden, bought a Unimate robot. It was used in the foundry to lift finished goods out of the casting moulds and then place them in a cooling bed.

Die-casting had been pioneered in USA, which is why Unimation were looking for willing users within this sector. Svenska Metallverken was Sweden's largest die casting foundry and robots were well suited to their production. Volvo was the foundry's most important customer. On behalf of Volvo, Svenska Metallverken manufactured, among other things, winders for windows, parts for the dashboard and flywheel housings.

The robot was chiefly to be used to replace the monotonous job of picking in and out. This process was also sped up, since the robot could handle parts even when they were hot.

In the beginning of the 1970s, Svenska Metallverken was bought by Gränges who then acquired more industrial robots.

The first spot-welding robots

In 1969, Unimation installed its first large spot-welding line. It consisted of 26 robots for spot-welding car bodies at General Motors. In 1972, they were involved in setting up the first European spot-welding line with robots at Fiat.

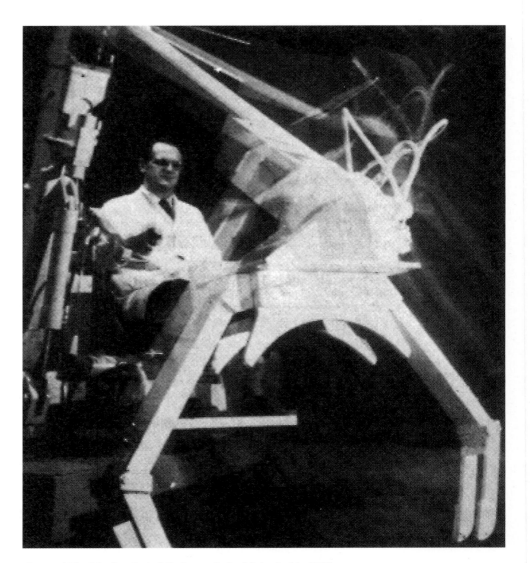

**General Electric developed their own industrial robot in 1967.
It was far too clumsy to work well.**

methods for robots in the fields of milling, drilling and thread cutting, mainly within the aviation industry.

Volvo was quick to use Unimate robots but, after the introduction of the T3, they chose to invest in the installation of a number of robots from Cincinnati Milacron in their factories in Torslanda and Olofström.

Development was slow

In 1973, there was a total of about 3,000 robots in operation around the world, of which a third were produced by Unimation. At that time, 71 companies worldwide manufactured industrial robots.

In the 1970s, more and more companies started using robots. However, development was not as fast as the robot manufacturers had hoped. A good example of this is the fact that Unimation did not show positive figures until 1975.

The Robot Institute of America, later renamed The Robot Industries Association (RIA), was founded in 1974. It is the only organisation of its kind in North America to focus exclusively on robots. Among its members are manufacturers of industrial robots and peripheral devices, companies dealing with system integration, end-users of robots and development companies within robot technology.

In 1977, the RIA founded "The Joseph F. Engelberger Award" for the most significant achievements in the use of robots.

3 | Scandinavian Initiatives

Trallfa, a Norwegian company manufacturing wheelbarrows at a factory in Stavanger, needed new spray painting equipment. This was brought to the fore by a bad working environment that made it difficult to recruit new workers.

In 1964, Ole Molaug, who was head of Jaerens Automasjonsselskap, had seen a newspaper article about the first Unimate robots that had been installed. The robot cost about 600,000 Norwegian crowns. Molaug suggested that Trallfa should try to make a cheaper robot for spray painting.

The owner and Managing Director of Trallfa, Nils Underhaug, jumped at the chance. Molaug maintained that he could build a robot that would cost no more than 15,000 Norwegian crowns. Under the management of Molaug, Trallfa ventured into the project. The engineer, Sverre Bergene, took on the mechanical side of things. They were now in unknown territory and countless numbers of problems began to pile up. As soon as one problem was solved, along came another. Nonetheless, the work proceeded and the project group did not give up.

Everything worked!

They presented the robot (which had been given the name "Ole") for the first time in connection with "Jaerdagen" in 1966. It was an electrohydraulic robot that could perform continuous movements and was very easy to program.

However, the robot was still not good enough to use for spray painting. Nevertheless, Nils Underhaug would not allow himself to be beaten by these technical problems and delays. In February 1967, it was at last time to run "Ole" in the spray painting plant. Now everything worked! The robot worked day after day, week after week and month after month. The investment led to a large increase in capacity at the spray painting plant. Besides the fact that the workforce could be reduced from five men to three, the quality of paintwork was better and savings were made, thanks to less paint being used.

Became a global product

The idea initially was to have a painting robot for their own use. It soon became obvious that the product had greater potential. The decision to produce a robot that could be sold on the world market was now taken.

The first Trallfa robot was shown in January 1969 at an exhibition celebrating the 50th anniversary of the Federation of Norwegian Industries. The robot attracted great attention.

In April 1969, the old prototype was taken out of operation at Trallfa and one of the new robots was installed in order to first test the machine under their own personal supervision to see how it worked. The evaluation was complete in October the same year and the first Trallfa robot for spray painting, named TR-2000, was delivered to Gustavsberg in Sweden

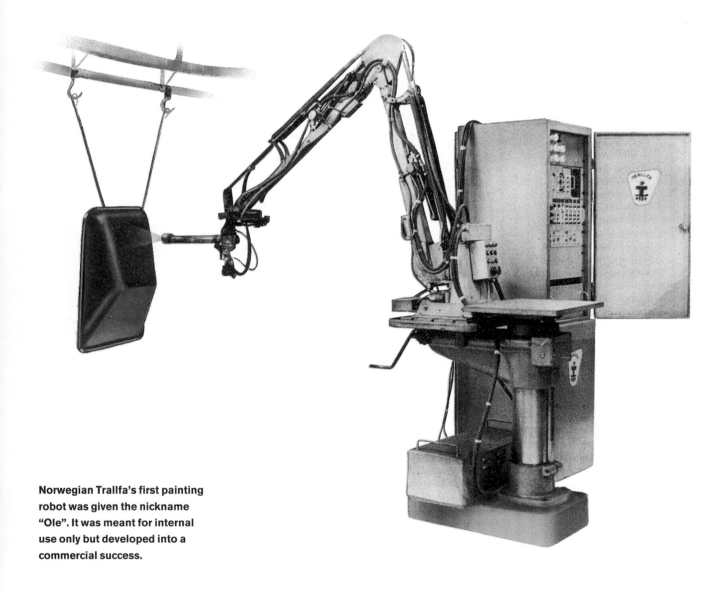

Norwegian Trallfa's first painting robot was given the nickname "Ole". It was meant for internal use only but developed into a commercial success.

where it was used for enamelling bathtubs and shower tubs.

It took just over five years from the first sketch to the first external delivery. A lot of energy and money had been invested along the way, so now it was important to earn a return on the investment. Trallfa made twenty robots in 1970 and the ball was rolling.

Kaufeldt the pioneer

Roland Kaufeldt started work as a nineteen year-old in the drawing office at LM Ericsson. At the end of the 1950s, he started his own company specialising in pneumatics. His factory was situated in Stuvsta, outside Stockholm.

Kaufeldt was a person full of integrity. He was not a person you would want to pick a fight with and he was choosy with whom he spoke. Kaufeldt did not have time to listen to long-winded people and he did not want to have anything to do with people who did not understand technology.

Afraid of his own robots

In the beginning of the 1970s, he produced his own pneumatic robot, which was sold mainly to the plastics industry. However, Roland Kaufeldt was worried about how the introduction of his robot would affect society and its development. He wrote a letter to the minister of industry at the time, Krister Wickman, warning of the consequences of his robot were it

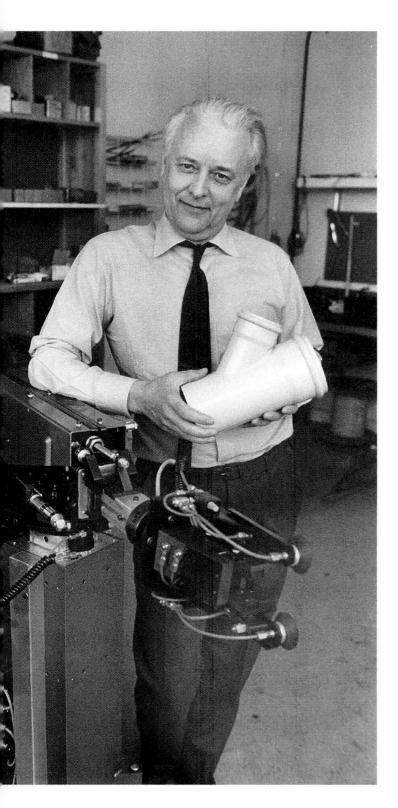

to be mass-produced. In the newspaper "Aftonbladet", he commented on his letter: The State must stop the import of labour in time. Industry is very interested in my invention. Instead of paying wages they want to buy my robot.

Bought by Monark

In 1971, the bicycle manufacturers Monark took over the robotics company Kaufeldt AB. Roland Kaufeldt continued working there but now as a consultant. Their assignment was to produce an automatic machine for constructing bicycle wheels. Monark was also to use Kaufeldt's robots in their production; one of them was used, amongst other things, for transferring pieces of tubing sideways to five different sta-

Roland Kaufeldt, one of the pioneers in the robot industry, developed his own pneumatic robot. His company was later sold to bicycle manufacturer Monark.

CHAPTER 3
Scandinavian initiatives

tions. Holes were made in the tube, it was stamped and, finally, it became the crank housing for a bike. By utilising the robot, several workstations could be combined into one.

Electrolux join the game

At the end of the 1960s, Electrolux, under the management of Hans Werthén, decided to increase automation in their factories producing household appliances. The production manager, Emil Andersson, was to carry out a comprehensive study in 1969. It showed that Electrolux needed 300 robots in total.

Electrolux began discussions with robot manufacturer Kaufeldt. They wanted him to produce a modular built robot for them. When Kaufeldt informed them he was unable to help, Electrolux chose to start manufacturing their own electropneumatically-controlled robots. Their robot was called MHU, Material Handling Unit, and it had a special feature that enabled it to tilt its arm downwards, which in some situations could replace an absolute vertical movement. Among other things, MHU was used for machine tending, assembling, surface treatment, checking and loading or unloading.

In 1971, the first MHU robot was installed in the Electrolux factory in Motala. The robot was used in the production of a tube component for absorption refrigerators.

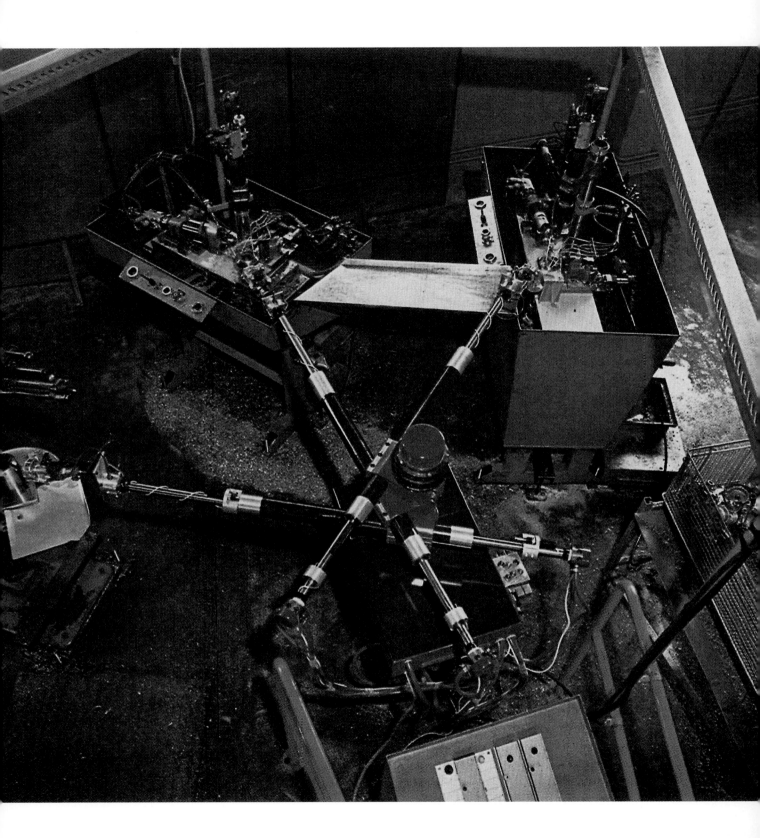

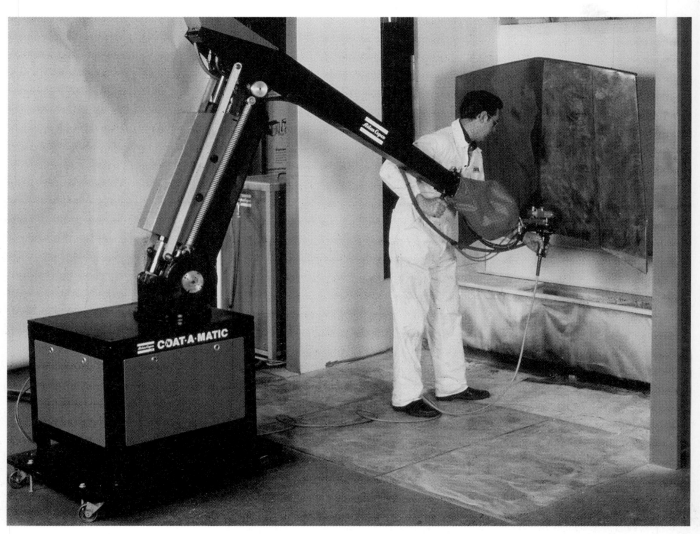

Atlas Copco had their own robot that was used for painting, the Coat-A-Matic.
In total, some 200 of these robots were delivered.

Electrolux continued its investment in the MHU robot and was the Swedish agent for the Unimate and Trallfa robots. By 1975, they had 75 robots in the factory in Motala.

Electrolux was very close to buying Unimation in the late 1970s, but another business deal intervened.

Esab and Atlas Copco

There were also other Swedish companies involved in the industrial robot industry. For example, ESAB built a robot in the middle of the 1970s that was used for arc welding. Using robots for arc welding came later than for spot-welding. This was because of problems controlling the robot and welding gun along a continuous joint with sufficient accuracy and correct speed.

Atlas Copco had their own robot, Coat-A-Matic, that was used for painting. Atlas Copco had bought the robot from the electronics company Retab who developed the basic machine, with Atlas Copco fine-tuning the control system. The robots were manufactured in a factory in Hammarby, Stockholm.

Atlas Copco was a large supplier to the automotive industry. Among other things, they manufactured and sold compressed air tools that could tighten nuts and bolts and surface treatment units. Atlas Copco delivered about 200 Coat-A-Matic robots in total. The robot was not only used for

painting but also for other kinds of spraying, for example ceramic coating on bathtubs and sanitary ware. Most of their customers were from Europe, the former Soviet Union and the USA. However, Coat-A-Matic was always number two after Trallfa and it was eventually discontinued. There are still around 40 Coat-A-Matic robots in operation around the world.

Robots in the shipbuilding industry

Kockums in Malmö led the way in the shipping industry when it came to introducing industrial robots. In 1974, the idea arose to use robots for welding hull sections. This was due to the large number of welded joints, which gave a troublesome environment for the welders to work in. The welding lengths were very short and the space around the joints was limited, so the welders had to work on their backs in the confined spaces. There was also a great risk that they would breathe large amounts of smoke.

Kockums started discussions with Unimation, who were to develop a light robot with five axles that was easy to handle and program. The result became the welding robot Apprentice.

Work was started on the prototype in 1976. The first welding attempts were carried out in the testing room at Danbury. An enquiry for developing suitable welding equipment for the robot went first to ESAB. However, they were not "hot" enough and the Finnish company Kemppi in Lahti became the designer of the welding equipment. In 1977, the robot was run together with the welding equipment for the first time and, in 1978, four robots were put into commission at the shipyard.

Unfortunately, the ship building industry went into a decline at the same time as the robot was fully developed. This meant that Kockums did not receive orders for large ships as before and robot automation did not become as big as it otherwise would have been. Nonetheless, the Apprentice robot became a big sales success for Unimation in the USA.

Finnish robots

The first two industrial robots in Finland were taken into operation in 1971. They were supplied by Electrolux and Unimation.

In 1976, the Finnish company Rosenlew began manufacturing their own industrial robots, which went under the name of Valco. This robot was later acquired by the company Wärtsilä, who were also to take over the American company GCA and create the company CIMCORP.

4 | Asea Create a Unique Robot

The first Unimate robot was installed at Asea in 1969. There were 25 Unimate robots in service in Asea's die-casting foundries in 1972.

ASEA OBTAINED ITS FIRST advanced multi-operational machine in 1962 and, after a couple of years, became the largest user of NC machines and advanced production techniques in Europe. They developed and marketed their own NC control systems; a predecessor to today's robot control systems. These NC systems were successively computerised from the end of the 1960s and interest for the development of new control systems has always been deeply rooted within Asea.

In 1969, Asea installed its first Unimate robot. The Swedish born MD at Unimation, Ted Lindbom, had been on at Asea boss Curt Nicolin for many years before he finally decided to invest in robots. Ted Lindbom and Curt Nicolin were namely good friends; a friendship that was formed in the 1950s after working together at Volvo Flygmotor with the development of jet motors to the aeroplane called "The Flying Barrel".

Good work environment and high productivity

Asea's development department was responsible for the introduction of robots in the company and it had obtained a sound knowledge of the technology. In 1972, twenty-five Unimate robots were used in Asea's die-casting foundry.

Industrial robots proved to be well suited to Asea's manufacturing plants. There were many hazardous jobs to be performed using die-casting machines and different kinds of injection moulding. The management want-

Curt Nicolin was the driving force behind the creation of the ASEA industrial robot.

CHAPTER 4
*Asea create
a unique robot*

ed to create a good work environment combined with high productivity.

The most successful installation was two Unimate robots used for assembling rotors for motors. The first one was used for putting together the rotors and the second was used to grind them. Thanks mainly to these industrial robots, Asea was able to reduce the processing time in that part of the factory from three weeks to 20 minutes!

Several of the Unimate robots were also used to handle parts between different machines.

Their very own industrial robot system

Curt Nicolin in Sweden was interested in manufacturing Unimate robots on licence but it was Electrolux that became sales representative for the Unimate robot in Scandinavia. Asea then chose to invest in the development of their own robots instead.

Björn Weichbrodt was recruited from General Electrics, where he had worked for nine years, to the position of Project Manager. He came to General Electrics as a young and green acoustics expert to take part in the development of quieter submarines for the US Department of Defense. When the defence contract expired, Weichbrodt was instead put in the automation department, where he was finally to become manager.

However, he had begun to think about returning home to Sweden and in the summer of 1971, Weichbrodt visited Asea to see if there were any

positions vacant. That same autumn, when Curt Nicolin had got the industrial robots plans moving, development manager Bengt Kredell was given the responsibility of starting such a venture. It was now up to him to find a project manager who was also a strong entrepreneur and dared to present new ideas. He then recalled the homesick automation expert,

Björn Weichbrodt, who had obtained 20 or so patents in the field of acoustics during his time at GE, proving that the 34 year-old possessed creative abilities.

In December 1971, Björn Weichbrodt moved into an empty office in Asea's hydraulic department. Initially, of course, everybody assumed that it would be a hydraulically powered industrial robot.

Hydraulic or electric?

Weichbrodt now started considering different robot concepts. Because Asea had never had robots in their range of products, it was high time for them to think of new angles of approach.

They worked on two concepts during the first stage, one with an electric drive system and one with a hydraulic drive system. They also worked on both tabletop and floor models. On April 6th 1972, Björn Weichbrodt put forward a proposal for a fully electrical robot to the management team headed by Curt Nicolin. The project received strong support from Asea's management, which had realised that the time was right for the industrial robot, despite the fact that many were focused on the development of nuclear power.

The idea of investing in an electric robot was not wrong for a company whose business concept was to develop the use of electric power. An important factor in the dignity of the project was the presence of Curt Nicolin in the management team. Three million Swedish crowns were set aside for pilot studies, which was a great deal of money then.

Handpicked development group

The pilot studies went well and in June 1972, the board at Asea made the historical decision to allow the development of their own industrial robot system.

First of all, a prototype was to be made. Björn Weichbrodt now moved to Asea's central development department, where he handpicked a group of 18 engineers with specialist knowledge in the fields of product technology, mechanical engineering and industrial electronics to work under his supervision. Six people under the leadership of Lars Stavmar worked with the mechanical side of things. There was also a large group, led by Leif Danielsen, that produced the control system including the new Intel 8008 based microcomputer. Included in the group was Göran Lundin, who played an important part in the development of the robot program. At this time, Intel was an unknown new company and at Asea, they were sceptical to their lasting power. Nonetheless, Asea put their trust in them. The control program just about fitted in 8 kb, compared with around 13 Megabytes today; that is to say 2000 times as much. Due to the necessity of pressing the program into such a limited memory, it was extremely compressed and complicated.

*Asea create
a unique robot*

Several new technical innovations

The industrial robot contained several new technical innovations. It was fully electrical, both the drive and the control systems, and it was anthropomorphic as well as being the first robot to be controlled by a microcomputer.

Its designer, Ove Kullborg, had originally drawn a five-axle robot where the grab arm moved horizontally and vertically in a traditional way and it was fitted with a rotating base. Björn Weichbrodt thought they should test the possibility of an anthropomorphic solution instead, i.e. that the arm function should be similar to that of a human being. This idea came from the robots that were used at GE to move refrigerators between the lines. Trallfa had also played with the idea of an anthropomorphic solution. Asea's designers now began to draw a robot with upper and lower arms with tie rod.

A compact gear

The choice of the Harmonic Drive planetary gear, which was fitted on axles 1–3, was another key feature that made the robot less clumsy. Harmonic Drive was extremely compact and provided a high gear ratio. The introduction of microprocessors in industrial robots was an important technical breakthrough. It was an exciting moment at the factory when the first microprocessors were installed. They had been flown there from In-

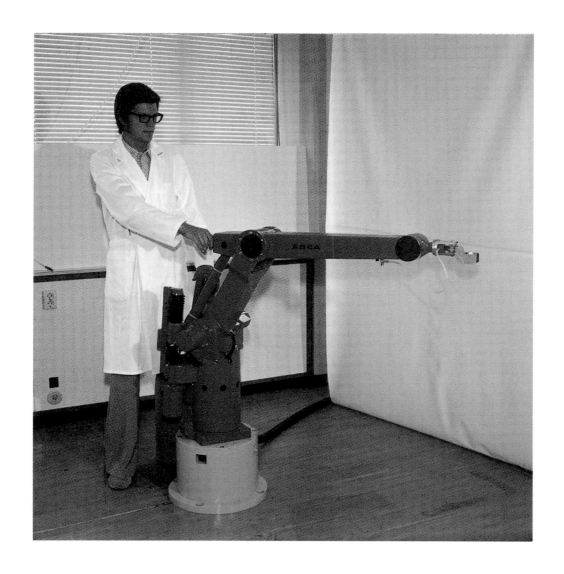

Designer Ove Kullborg testing the first prototype of the IRB 6. He had first designed a five-axle robot on which the grab arm moved horizontally and vertically in a traditional way. However, he chose an anthropomorphic solution.

tel in the USA. It was the first time that microprocessors were used in an Asea product and actually the first chip Intel had ever delivered.

During the course of product development, the drive system was changed from a stepping motor to a DC motor from GEC Alsthom. The stepping motor had proved to be too sensitive to overloading. The DC motor was fast thanks to the low moment of inertia. It was also cheaper and a DC motor was simply better suited to robots.

Worked on Christmas Day

Design responsibility was shared mainly between Ove Kullborg and his colleague Bengt Nilsson. Kullborg was responsible for the ballscrews and the drive for axle 1, while Nilsson was responsible for the upper and lower arms. There was a positive entrepreneurial spirit within the development group and work was so intense that, at times, it could go on around the clock. It was the type of spirit that can usually only be found among the self-employed. They even worked on Christmas Day 1972 to avoid delaying the robot.

The first model

The first model was presented to the board of Asea in February 1973. Despite lacking technical finesse, to the untrained eye, the robot appeared to be finished. Björn Weichbrodt demonstrated how the robot worked in front of the board members by allowing it to move blocks back and forth.

The board, with Swedish financier Marcus Wallenberg at the forefront, was impressed and decided to continue its development. It was now full steam ahead. The industrial robot was to start being produced in series and Curt Nicolin pushed for the first units to be sold before the end of the year.

In connection with this decision, Weichbrodt's group moved to the electronics division where a special department was set up for industrial robots. The people working in product development felt good about not being part of a large company bureaucracy. Instead, they were allowed to function as a separate, self-governing department that was responsible for their own results from an early stage. It took the group no more than ten months from the first decision to a working prototype.

IRB 6 a success

In October 1973, Asea exhibited a prototype of a robot they called IRB 6, which meant a lifting capacity of six kilos, at a transport and handling trade fair at the Hotel Foresta in Stockholm. The highlight of the fair was when it made its first movements.

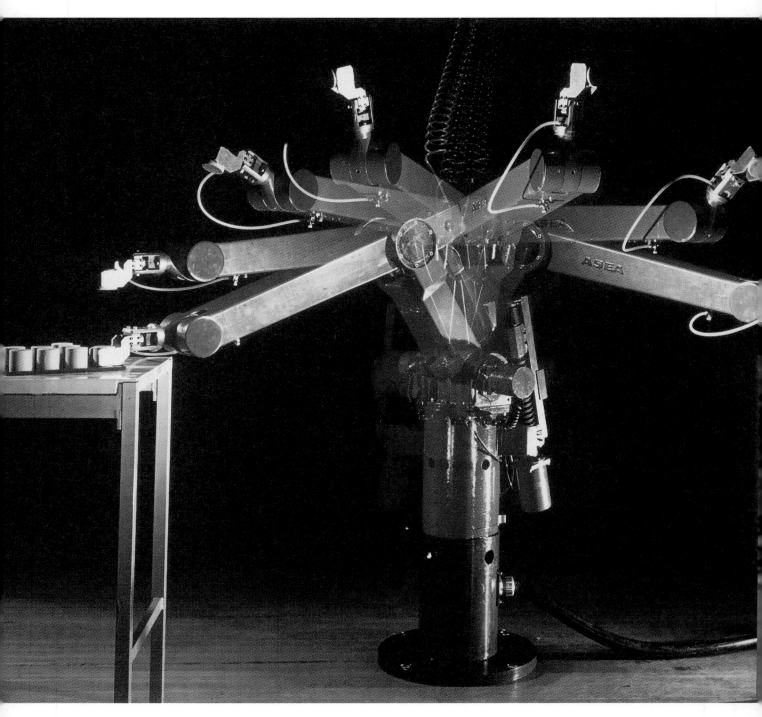

Movement of the anthropomorphic industrial robot IRB 6 with arm functions resembling those of a human being.

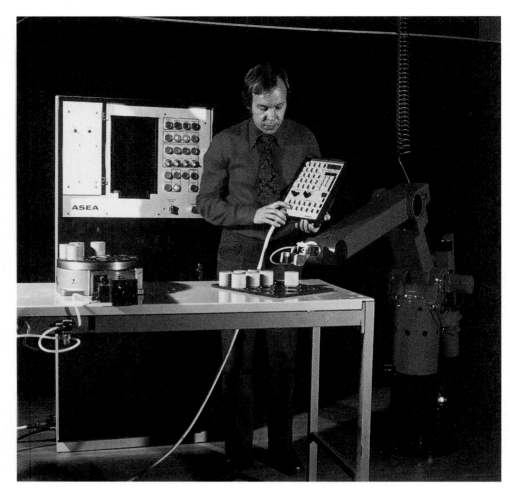

A microprocessor from Intel was used in the control system for the IRB 6. The control program took up 8 kilobytes of memory, which can be compared with the 13 Megabytes of today – 2000 times the size.

Asea had a unique product but who was to manufacture the robot? Since it was a totally new niche for them, it was not possible to include it in their production along with their other well-established products.

Ove Kullborg travelled around Sweden trying to find an Asea owned company that could manufacture industrial robots. He was in Härnösand and Helsingborg, among other places, but none of the workshops had the required machine park, so he decided to return to Asea in Västerås where the management had the existing electronics division take care of production. The control system is the most expensive and most important

CHAPTER 4

*Asea create
a unique robot*

part of an industrial robot, so this decision proved to be a good long-term solution.

Magnusson buys the first robot

The first three robots were taken into operation in January 1974. Two of them were used in the company's own factory. One of them handled breakers at Asea in Ludvika and the other unloaded plastic mouldings in the machine shop in Västerås.

The feeling within Asea was that the first external customer would be another large Swedish company but this was not the case. The first Asea robot was sold to the Magnusson engineering company in Genarp, a small firm with 20 employees and a small workshop in southern Sweden. Leif Jönsson, son-in-law to the founder Allan Magnusson, ran the company. They produced stainless steel pipes for the food industry; the Magnusson-bend was a well-known term in the industry, meaning that a pipe could be bent in a 90-degree angle.

Leif Jönsson was a technically curious man with a very positive attitude when it came to finding new solutions. The same year he bought the robot, he also bought the company's first computer.

He first came in contact with the IRB 6 during a dinner, where a representative for Asea gave an account of the development of the robot and the project they were working on, which was almost complete but for the

CHAPTER 4

*Asea create
a unique robot*

installation of the microprocessor. The day after hearing this, Leif Jönsson rang and spoke to a surprised salesman at Asea and ordered a robot.

Widened the bottleneck

The task of the industrial robot at Magnusson's in Genarp was to grind bent pipes on a sanding belt and then wax and polish them. The grinding and polishing was not a very pleasant job and had earlier caused a bottle-neck in production. At that time they used wax, which did not exactly con-tribute to a good working environment.

Some people consider it daring of Jönsson to act as a "guinea pig". None-theless, one should remember that Leif Jönsson was well aware that Asea had invested a lot of prestige in the robot project and would back him up if there were any problems. Certainly, there were a few teething troubles. The robot lacked a sixth axle that was to be added later, and a few cables had to be re-routed. One problem that took Jönsson and his fellow work-ers a long time to solve was introducing the peripheral equipment needed for the robot to increase productivity. The initial programming also took time. The pay off time, however, was not especially long, thanks to the in-tensive use of the robot and the widening of the bottleneck in production.

The first unmanned factory

In 1975, Jönsson was one of the first in the world to operate an unmanned factory around the clock, seven days a week. The challenge involved daring to allow the robots to work without any supervision. At the end of the working day, a pallet of unpolished bent pipes was brought forward. The robot was then able to pick and polish pipes for four hours. Leif Jönsson would then change the pallet when he went out to walk the dog in the evening and the robot could continue working for another four hours. There were a few incidents in the beginning, but reliability was continually being improved.

The first industrial robot that Leif Jönsson bought was in operation around the clock for ten years until Asea repurchased it in connection with their 100-year anniversary to be used as a museum exhibit. Before it became a museum piece, Jönsson's robot had performed 70,000 work-hours. It has now had several successors in the factory and the IRB 6 robots bought by Magnusson in 1975 are still being used there.

Aptitude for arc welding

It was not initially clear what the newly developed IRB 6 would mainly be used for since the market was so undeveloped. According to the instructions, the robot had been designed to pick things and also to move from one point to another along curves. It is true to say that the IRB 6 was suited for handling materials but that function was not the main reason for the success that followed. Instead, it was to be the robot's great aptitude for process applications such as arc welding, welding and deburring that eventually gave the positive sales figures.

The IRB 6 was a success and resulted in Asea forming a department for workshop automation with Björn Weichbrodt as head. They sold 17 robots the first year and 25 the second. The IRB managed to carry out many more tasks than the competing robots could at that time. Their customers gained advantages in the form of higher speed, higher repetitive accuracy and simpler programming. The patented linkage system was the foundation for the high repetitive accuracy.

The design of the IRB 6 became the model for robot development during the 1970s. It is the most copied industrial robot in the world and it is an interesting piece of industrial history.

Since Asea's robot group had started out on the right foot, the next model, the IRB 60, was introduced as early as 1975. It was also a pioneer as not many people believed it possible to make such a large robot with an

The IRB 6 just before it was discontinued in 1991. The model existed for 17 years, which is something of a record in industrial robot circles.

electric drive system. Both these two robot models were around for a long time and were included in the product range until 1991. Altogether, they produced 7,000 IRB 6 and sold 1,900 IRB 60. The IRB 60 was used for mainly materials handling. Another milestone during the 1970s was when Asea Robotics in 1978 introduced the first adaptive robot that could communicate with a parent computer. This initiated the development towards CIM, Computer Integrated Manufacturing.

Helped along by mass media

Just as Joseph Engelberger received help from the media in the beginning, Asea also succeeded in increasing interest in this way. Among other things, the marketing people at Asea had a robot draw the King's portrait in 30 seconds in connection with his visit to the robot workshop and he also attended a course to learn how the robots worked. On another occasion, the IRB 6 played the synthesiser at Olympia in Paris. Many articles were written and the TV broadcast pictures.

Many industrial robots were
also installed at ASEA. These
two were used for assembling
contactors in the S-division
and were called "Adam" and
"Eve".

CHAPTER 4

*Asea create
a unique robot*

The robot became a symbol for everything that changed life in the workplace. Not all Swedes were positive to these newfangled machines, however, and it resulted in a long mass-media debate. There were discussions on whether a machine with movements that partly resembled those of a human being could not only be seen as an aid but also as a direct threat to the workers and their job security.

Invest in export

During the first years, most of the Asea robots were installed in the company's own factories. Nonetheless, Asea did not see Sweden as its main market for robots and an energetic investment in export was started. The first centre for robots was established in Germany in 1975 and was followed by similar centres in many other countries. These centres were allocated resources for marketing, sales, service, training and technical planning. In other words, an entire organisation to solve the customer's production problems. Of course, Asea had realised that the robot was only one part of an entirety.

Just as Joseph Engelberger received help from the media in the beginning, Asea also succeeded in increasing interest in this way. The robot became a symbol for the changing way of life in the workplace.

This is why they offered a "functional package". During the 1970s, Asea developed work methods for deburring, grinding and polishing.

Despite the good start, the company's financial experts did not directly appreciate the profitability of the Asea robot division. The development work and marketing actually cost a lot of money. In the beginning, they sold about 100 robots a year, which was not quite enough for a good result. Björn Weichbrodt admitted that it took longer than expected but, just as for Unimation, it took a while before the robot business became profitable. It was 1978 before Asea's figures for the industrial robots were the right colour.

5 | Robot Fever in Japan

JAPANESE INDUSTRY started with automatic assembly as early as the beginning of the 1960s. Companies such as Matsushita and Toshiba, who mass-produced products like fluorescent tubes, light bulbs and dry batteries, led the way in the introduction of automatic processes on their assembly lines. Fujitsu and NEC were also among the first to have automatic assembly machines for the production of relays.

The fast growing Japanese automotive industry was also caught in the wave of automation. Spark plugs, bumpers and front wheels were car parts that could quite easily be assembled automatically.

Calling such machines industrial robots is saying too much, they were rather various kinds of manipulators. They worked nonetheless and brought about an increase in production and a decrease in costs.

Engelberger and Engellau visit Japan

Interest for industrial robots increased in Japan at the end of the 1960s. An important milestone was when Joseph Engelberger was invited to Japan to hold lectures on robots. During a week-long stay in Japan, he was able to talk about the advantages of robots to 700 business executives. He also held similar lectures in his own country but there, Engelberger did not have more than a handful of listeners.

The visit resulted in Unimation giving the Japanese company, Kawasaki Heavy Industries, a licence to build Unimate robots in 1968. Selling the

CHAPTER 5
Robot fever in Japan

Industrial robots were just the thing for the Japanese who had a positive basic attitude to robotisation.

licence was very important for Unimation, whose owners had started to complain about the lack of profits. That the Japanese wanted to use their robots gave them hope for the future.

Johan Jakob Engellau, who led the Electrolux robot operations, also went over to Japan and, like Engelberger, he entered into a licensing agreement with Kawasaki for the manufacture of MHU robots in Japan.

Robot fever was now spreading in Japan. The Japanese were very quick

to apply the new technology, which meant that they could increase productivity and take new market shares.

Just right for the Japanese

When it came to robotics, everything was perfect for the Japanese. There were not enough people to produce due to the high economic growth,
which, at the end of the 1960s, was an average twelve percent per year. The

demand for manpower was much higher than the supply.

The relationship between management and workers was good in Japan and the owners thought long-term and were not only chasing quick profits, which is often the case in the USA and, to a certain extent, even in Europe. Japanese robot manufacturers often constituted one part of a larger group of companies. In most cases, other units within the group developed integrated circuits and computers. They were able to transfer important knowledge to their robot manufacturing "siblings".

Another success factor was the Japanese government who, in many different ways, sponsored co-operation between the robotics industry, manufacturing companies wanting to invest money in the new technology and universities.

In addition, it is worth noting that the positive attitude of the Japanese towards robots was partly due to the popular Japanese comic figure "Astro Boy", a kind and cute robot that fought for world peace. He appeared for the first time in 1953 in a Japanese comic and was as popular in Japan as Mickey Mouse and Donald Duck were in the West.

The first robotics organisation

Japan was first in the world to establish a robotics organisation in 1971. It was called the Japan Industrial Robot Association JIRA. Its purpose was to actively support the development of the Japanese robotics industry.

JARA, as the organisation was later called, was to be an important driving force in encouraging more Japanese companies to invest in robots.

Many of Japan's top company heads were involved in this organisation. Its first Chairman was the Managing Director of Mitsubishi.

Japanese copies of the IRB

Of all the components in the Asea IRB 6 robot, only the linkage system could be patented. Consequently, it did not take long before copies started appearing in Japan. When it was suddenly reported that there were half a dozen "copies" of the IRB 6, the people at Asea naturally became disappointed and dismayed. Nonetheless, they could only accept that their patent had not provided them with enough protection. The most sophisticated "copy" was manufactured by the company Yaskawa.

Fanuc and Siemens

Fujitsu-Fanuc, the leading Japanese manufacturer of NC machines, produced its first industrial robot in 1975. Three years earlier, they had started co-operating with the German company Siemens.

Fanuc's range of robots originally consisted of robots that were used for handling materials for NC machines. They soon became involved in the production of assembly robots.

Fanuc, whose factory is beautifully situated by Mount Fuji, was origi-

Fanuc's robots were given a pronounced colour profile. Everything from the workers' overalls to the industrial robots was yellow.

Seiuemon Inaba, head of Fanuc, wore a watch that went ten times faster than normal. This was his way of symbolising his wish for faster product development.

nally run by the engineer Seiuemon Inaba. He chose to give the company a very pronounced colour profile. The walls of the building, the robots, the overalls, the apartments, everything was painted in yellow.

Another one of Inaba's distinctive features was his watch, which went ten times faster than a normal watch. This was a symbol for how fast he wanted product development to go.

Sought international partners

The oil crisis of 1973 put the raw-material meagre country under immense pressure and, among other things, this led to demands on increasing productivity even more. The Japanese companies searched frantically for ways to cut their costs. The problem was often solved by an increase in automation.

However, the Japanese were cautious when it came to exporting their industrial robots. To start with, Japanese robot manufacturers found it quite difficult to adjust their products to the markets of North America and Europe. To succeed on this front, they sought strong international partners.

Increased research resources

Research investments were increased greatly and, in 1980, research within the field of robotics was being carried out at about 85 universities and other state research institutions across the whole of Japan. The number of research institutions had doubled since 1974. FMC (Flexible Manufacturing Complex) was one of the larger research projects. It started in 1977 and lasted for six years. The aim of the project was to develop new flexible robot systems for automatic manufacturing of machine parts in small series.

19,000 industrial robots

Between 1970–1975, the production of industrial robots increased on average by 18% per year and, between 1975–80, the increase accelerated to about 40%.

In 1980, 19,000 industrial robots were manufactured in Japan by approximately 150 different robot manufacturers. Kawasaki was the largest, producing just over 600 robots a year. Right on their heels was Yaskawa followed by a whole chain of other manufacturers such as Hitachi, Mitsubishi Heavy Industries, Kobe Steel and Fanuc.

Different types of applications within the manufacturing industry such as pressing, processing and welding were most common. The electronics industry had also started using robots for assembly.

The enthusiasm for robotics was still huge. Even on the streets, people talked about them as if they were a blessing, which was not particularly strange; the motto of the robot industry, "no workers have lost their jobs through being replaced by a robot" still rang true.

Nachi was one of about 150 Japanese manufacturers of industrial robots operational in 1980.

6 | Europe Awakens

APART FROM THE ENERGETIC initiatives taken in Scandinavia, Europe awoke quite late to industrial robots. In Europe, there was not the same type of bank-controlled conglomerates as in Japan. These had many legs to stand on and the good insight the banks had into robotic companies made financing easier, reducing the demand for a return on investments.

Another reason for the more cautious attitude towards robots in Europe was the fact that there was no shortage of labour there.

There was not the same need to create "compact" robotised factories. By tradition, large and roomy factories had been built in Europe.

The European industrial structure was largely based on small and medium sized companies that manufactured products in small series. During the first ten years that industrial robots were on the market, they were not suited to this kind of manufacturing. It took far too long to programme between each new product.

Kuka robots

Nevertheless, there were companies on the European continent that joined the robotics industry in the beginning of the 1970s. One was the engineering company Kuka in Augsburg. They started their robot career by installing a welding line, equipped with industrial robots, for their own use. Kuka acted first as a dealer for international robot manufacturers and later, they created their own robot model for spot-welding in the auto-

There was plenty of available labour in Europe. Therefore, the necessary interest for robotising production was lacking.

German Kuka started manufacturing industrial robots in the early 70s. They constructed their own model of spot-welding robot for the automotive industry.

motive industry. Up until 1983, they had produced 1,200 robots, of which 90% went to the automotive industry. In the beginning of the 1980s, Kuka also ventured into assembly robots.

Car companies manufacture their own robots

The pioneer among robot users in the automotive industry was Daimler Benz. They were using robots for spot-welding as early as 1971 on the Mercedes S-model at their factory in Sindelfingen.

During the 1970s, the car manufacturers Volkswagen and Renault built their own robots for internal use. They were mainly used for welding. Renault also began to market them on the external market.

In 1983, Volkswagen began using robots for final assembly for the first time. This was when they were building the second-generation Golf in the newly built "Hall 54" in the Volkswagen works in Wolfsburg. At these works, they manufactured 2,400 cars a day. As they worked in two shifts, this meant that a new car was churned out every 16 seconds. In "Hall 54", they were using around 40 assembly robots.

In 1983, Volkswagen manufactured another 300 robots for their own use. Altogether at this time, they had 1,200 industrial robots in use. The Volkswagen works were at that time busy trying to produce a robot that worked with two parallel arms. The robot was a welder and a holder at the same time. This finesse meant that they could avoid expensive fixtures.

Not without controversy

The newspaper headlines about factories becoming increasingly robotised were not without controversy in Europe. The new technology made it possible to increase productivity per employee by approximately 5% per year, without increasing the workforce. It was estimated that each robot replaced somewhere between 1.4 and 1.6 workers. In assembly work, the figures were somewhere between 4 and 6 workers. This was at a time when many countries in Europe were fighting high unemployment. In Germany in 1984, for example, there were approximately 2.5 million people unemployed.

Robot automation led to some new occupational groups. The jobs were more in the area of checking and supervision. New job openings were created at subcontractors working in the field of electronic control engineering.

30 or so manufacturers

In 1983, there were a total of 30 or so manufacturers of industrial robots in West Germany. Altogether, during that year, they produced 2,000 robots. Industrial robots were mainly used within the machine industry, electronics industry and automotive industry. When it came to the machine industry, Kuka and Zahnrad were the largest. The Zahnrad factory, which was located in Friedrichhafen, had been manufacturing industrial robots since 1976.

Renault in France developed their own robots for manufacturing cars. They also started to turn towards the external market.

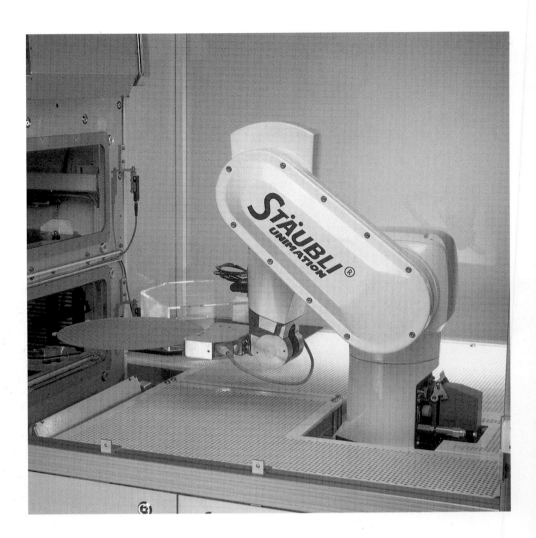

MANTEC, a subsidiary of Siemens in Erlagen, dominated the electronics industry. They had previously manufactured robots for Fanuc on licence but now had their own models.

Within the car industry, the Volkswagen works was number one.

In the beginning of the 1980s, several other German robot manufacturers appeared on the scene. Ottenser Eisenwerk in Hamburg began to produce robots for heavy lifting in 1981. Reis in Bernburg, who normally manufactured hydraulic presses for die-casting, began to produce industrial robots in 1982; their most important product was to be an assembly robot. In 1983, the company Behr in Ingersheim began manufacturing spray-painting robots.

Comau develops the press robot

The Italian company Fiat had used Unimate robots for spot-welding since 1972. The bodywork department in the factory in Turin, which went under the name of Comau, was given the assignment to develop their own robot system. The first hydraulically controlled industrial robot of theirs to see the light of day in 1978 was christened Polar.

In 1982 came Comau's first electrically controlled robot, Smart. Three years later, Comau made a technical breakthrough. This took place when they were automating the manual feed of materials to the presses in the Fiat factory. This resulted in the first press robot on the market, with the capacity to feed an entire line in a car factory. The Smart 6.30P robot was capable of transporting six to twelve pieces per minute. In 1988, Comau became a separate division within Fiat responsible for robot manufacturing.

In 1974, the Italian company Olivetti constructed the two-armed SIG-MA robot. This was a portal robot that was used for fitting electronic components onto circuit boards and parts for typewriters. The SIGMA project was led by Antonio d'Auria and Mario Salmon.

At the beginning of the 1980s, many small, specialised companies joined in the "game". A new group was made up of system integrators. They were to be called OEM (Original Equipment Manufacturer) companies and their business concept was to adapt existing robots to system solutions.

Up and down

It could be said that the industrial robot made its big breakthrough in Europe during the latter part of the 1970s. The annual rate of growth at that time was about 30%.

In 1986, the recently rising trend turned due to a decline in the automotive industry. The demand for robots decreased dramatically in many European countries and remained at a low level until 1988. It was in 1988 that the car industry began to invest again. In Europe and America, they had discovered that the Japanese investment in robotised spot-welding produced a more consistent quality and, therefore, welding became a prioritised area. Welding was, and still is, the most common area of use for robots in Europe. Nonetheless, the European automotive industry was far behind the Japanese when it came to robotics. In Japan, they use twice as many robots per manufactured car.

At the end of the 1980s, there was a rapid growth in Europe in the field of assembly. One phenomenon worth noting in particular was the plastics industry in Great Britain, which invested a great deal of effort into robotics.

Italian Comau, a division of the Fiat group, has manufactured industrial robots since 1978.

The European market

During the last decade of the twentieth century, the largest robotics companies on the European market were ABB, Fanuc, Yaskawa, (Motoman) Kuka, Comau and Renault Automation/ACMA. In the group following them, Closs and Reis of Germany, French-Swiss Stäubli and many small manufacturers were fighting for the throne. ABB Robotics was more than twice as big as its closest rival.

Fanuc was a strong challenger. They were chosen, for example, as main supplier to several of General Motors' factories in Europe as well as the new Nissan factories in Great Britain. However, Fanuc had difficulty in establishing itself on the European market for welding robots, which was soundly claimed by others. It was easier for them to gain attention for Japanese painting, gluing and material handling robots.

The strength of the European manufacturers was that they began thinking in terms of system solutions to a greater degree than the Japanese did. In Austria, there was also IGM Robotersysteme that was started in 1967 by two former engineers at Siemens, Günther Kloimüller and Frans Vokurka.

Research and development

West German robot research was concentrated to a few of the reputable Fraunhofer institutes, with the Institute for Production and Automation (IPA) in Stuttgart at the fore. IPA developed, among other things, a mobile robot system in co-operation with the company Jungheinrich in Hamburg.

In the middle of the 1980s, one of Germany's most important areas of research was sensors. Above all, they tried to develop an optical system with short processing times. In this case, the Fraunhofer institutes worked closely with the companies Siemens and Bosch.

The availability of semiconductor diodes opened up a new and interesting range of uses for sensors. Two different kinds of sensor systems are needed for an industrial robot, internal and external. The internal one controls the status of the robot, i.e. position, speed, torque, voltage and current. In addition, an external system is needed to read the surroundings, i.e. distance, position, orientation, speed and classification of the object.

The reason for so much time and effort being put into sensor development was that the lack of advanced sensors was hindering the development and growth of industrial robots. The need for improved sensors was especially great in connection with sorting, testing, finishing and assembly.

In West Germany, they experienced particularly difficult problems when using robots for finishing treatment, deburring and polishing. There were also occurrences of engineering companies buying new robots and dismantling them because they did not meet their quality requirements; this problem was also due to faults in the sensors.

It was therefore important to develop and improve optical systems. Seeing robots were in demand for visual tests, optical measuring, positioning and parts identification.

Communist robots

In the former Soviet Union, research in industrial robots was started in the beginning of the 1960s by a group of researchers at the University of Moscow, under the leadership of the academy member, I. Artobolevsky.

The development of robot prototypes was carried out at the Institute for Aircraft Technology (LIAP), in Leningrad. Professor M. Ignatiev led this work, which was started in 1966.

In 1969, they presented the prototypes for the first Soviet robots UM-1T, which was heat protected, and UM-1P, which was dirt protected.

The first robot used in industry was installed in 1971 at the drop forging works in Serpuchov. It was tested thoroughly and it was not until 1974 that the next one was installed, this time in a factory for manufacturing mechanical equipment in Kovrov. Installations subsequently increased and, in 1980, the number of industrial robots and advanced manipulators had reached 6,000. A couple of hundred of them had been imported.

Asea Robotics also sold manufacturing licences for IRB 6 to Poland at the end of the 1970s. This was important to Asea Robotics, who needed money to motivate a continued development of robots and to maintain their initiative. It was also an important step forward for Polish industry, which was in dire need of becoming more efficient.

A real robot ideology

In the Soviet Union, just as in Japan, there was a lack of industrial workers. This applied mainly to the European part of the country and there was no clash of interest whatsoever between the communist ideology and industrial robots. Noting what Lenin had to say gave the "friends" of industrial robots support for their argument.

"The progress of technology must involve machines taking over ever more manual labour from humans. The more technology is developed, the less humans shall be burdened with physical work", thought Lenin.

These thoughts formed the foundation of the Soviet Union's industrial planning. Workers were to be spared from doing harmful, monotonous and strenuous work.

Transfer of workers

Industrial robots were given plenty of attention in the five-year plan that was passed in 1981 and reading between the lines, almost all Soviet industry was to be robotised. Courses would be pursued at around 30 different high schools, around 50 institutes would carry out robot research and many robots would be manufactured so that hundreds of thousands of in-

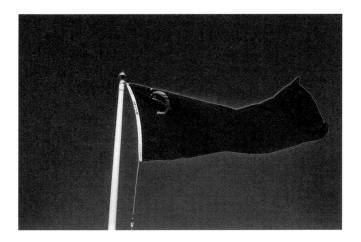

The ideology of communism and industrial robots did not clash. Studying what Lenin had to say gave the "friends" of industrial robots support for their argument.

dustrial workers that performed simple manual tasks could be transferred to more qualified work. The initial intention was an automation of the Soviet car industry, which mass-produced Lada and VAZ among other things.

With hindsight, we now know it did not turn out that way but, nonetheless, it is still interesting to study the large-scale plans.

Technically inferior

At the beginning of the 1980s, there were approximately 200 different Soviet robot models and around 40 of these were mass-produced. Most of them, however, were technically inferior to those made in the West. The majority were pneumatically driven and had a capacity of around 10 kilos.

There were also quite a few hydraulically driven robots that could handle up to 50 kilos, as well as a small number that were electrically operated.

It was difficult to obtain fast control systems with high-capacity memory in the Soviet Union. It was also difficult to get the electrical motors in working order. The dimensions of the robots were much too big in relation to their lifting capacity. In the beginning of the 1980s, they imported some Hungarian control systems, which eased the situation somewhat.

The economic life span was also relatively short; 3–5 years compared to 8–10 years in the West. One third of the 50,000 robots produced in the

Soviet Union between 1981 and 1985 produced less than an hour's work and were just standing in workshops, left to rust.

It was not easy to position robots in the old industries, which were not at all designed for automation. The products being manufactured were not designed to be handled automatically either, which was a problem experienced by most companies using industrial robots. Other East European countries such as Czechoslovakia, Rumania and Bulgaria also expressed great interest in developing their own industrial robots. They continued with their own designs as well as co-operating with European and Japanese companies for licensing. Several factories were established with large target volumes. However, the economic crisis and demand for maintaining sufficiently high quality were factors that halted this progress.

7 New Owners and New Partners

Percy Barnevik (here talking to Björn Weichbrodt) identified the growing robot market and succeeded in blowing life into it in the late eighties.

PERCY BARNEVIK TOOK OVER as CEO for Asea in 1980 and during his first year, he carried out a comprehensive study of the company. With a ten year background within Sandvik's tool operations, he saw enormous possibilities both in the automotive industry and in other industries.

Once he had started, Barnevik could see that Asea was technically advanced but that sales had only increased slowly during the 1970s. Priority was now given to more salesmen and "Robot Centers" in different countries, for demonstrations and customer training. Within the Wallenberg sphere, which owned Asea, there were three large manufacturers of industrial robots, Asea, Electrolux and Esab. Old Marcus Wallenberg was supposed to have said, "Robots are the future. One company should take care of them."

Side by side

Esab had delivered their first welding robot in 1974. They co-operated with Asea, who manufactured the robot, while Esab made the station into a turnkey production solution. They also worked together to develop the robot market for arc welding. Barnevik's analysis concluded that Esab Robotics and Asea Robotics should remain as separate organisations but continue to co-operate with each other.

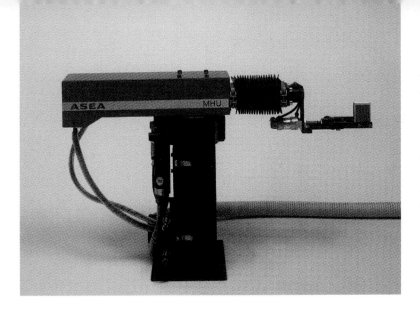

The MHU robot was incorporated in the Asea sphere in 1981. However, it was not long before Asea completely abandoned the production of the MHU to focus entirely on the IRB series.

Companies join forces

However, things were different with Asea Robotics and the Electrolux robot division. Barnevik saw only one solution and that was for the companies to join forces. But which of them had the greatest potential for the future? Electrolux, with their pneumatically controlled robots and access to Unimate robots, had a much larger share of the market, while Asea's electrically controlled robots were judged to possess a higher level of technology.

The merger became fact in 1981, with the forces concentrated to Asea in Västerås. Production of the MHU robot was moved in 1983 from Stockholm to Västerås. However, it did not take long before Asea completely abandoned production of the MHU and focused their attention on producing the IRB range. Björn Weichbrodt observes that the merger was not really a good solution. The two companies had been working with such completely different products, both in technology and price, that it was never a successful merger.

Göran Ridderström, who had earlier worked with the development of the MHU robots, took over the operation and now runs it under his own management as MHU Robotics in Täby.

Asea's takeover of the Norwegian company Trallfa, in 1985, went off without a hitch. Their painting robots and Asea's industrial robot program complemented each other in a way that was beneficial to both.

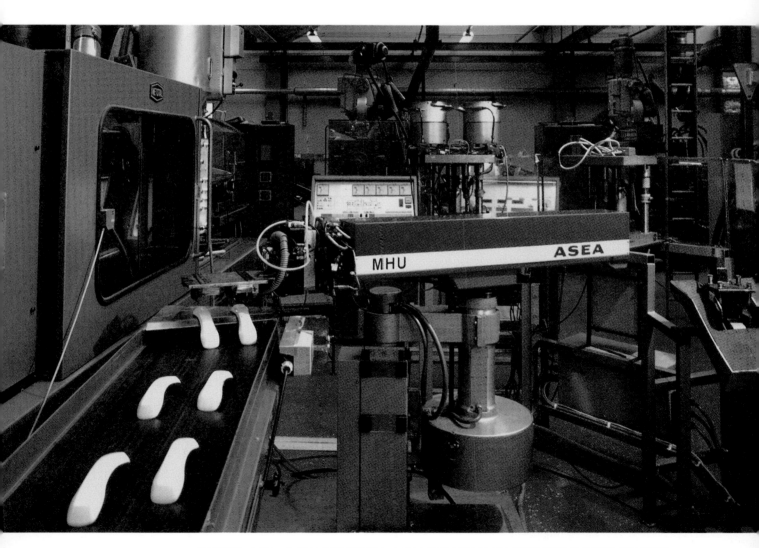

An **MHU**-senior working with telephone manufacturing at one of the Telia factories. The MHU robot was exceptional because it could tilt its arm down, a feature that could sometimes replace a separate vertical movement.

Although Barnevik preached profitability, it was growth and increased market shares that became gospel for the robots during the first half of the 1980s when there was an enormous increase in sales and Asea became established among the world leaders.

Barnevik also regarded robots as an important profile product and sometimes joked about Asea being better known in wider circles as a robot company rather than an electrotechnical company.

Disaster for Unimation

When the robot market stagnated in the middle of the 1980s, there was turbulence among the robot manufacturers. Some companies disappeared completely and a number of important acquisitions took place.

There were several prospective buyers of Unimation, whose owners had run into financial difficulties. Among the bidders were Asea, Westinghouse, Litton and General Electric. Joseph Engelberger would have preferred to see Asea take over Unimation. However, he could not make this decision on his own and the shareholders pushed for Westinghouse, who made the highest bid, to be allowed to buy Unimation. This took place in 1983 and was a classic example of an unsuccessful attempt at merging an entrepreneur-oriented organisation and a large company with a phlegmatic decision-making process. Engelberger, however, did

The Americans were good at inventing but did not manage to change in time when the market matured.

not emerge empty-handed and was able to buy himself a large yacht, on which he spent a lot of time until his "quarantine" was over and he could continue to develop new robots under his own management. He then made up his mind to always own a boat with a footage higher than his age.

Westinghouse stayed with hydraulic control, despite the fact that market demand was increasingly switching to electrically controlled robots. In 1984, for example, Chrysler removed 124 Unimate robots from their factory in Windsor, Ontario, and replaced them with electrically controlled robots.

One of the reasons Westinghouse continued with the hydraulic concept for such a long time was the price. Electrically controlled robots were much more expensive than the hydraulic ones. However, the profit was eventually eaten up by running costs, which were about twice as high for a hydraulic robot.

Kawasaki broke its collaboration with Unimation in 1986 and started its own manufacturing in Detroit. Kawasaki felt uncertain as to which direction Unimation was really going.

That same year, Westinghouse finally introduced a large electric robot, PUMA 760, which was to replace Unimate. However, the final dash was made much too late and it all ended in disaster. Unimation was sold in 1983 for 108 million dollars and in 1988, when it was bought by Stäubli, the price had gone down to 5 million dollars. The company had been drained of its expertise.

Far too complicated

Prab was also forced to close down its large industrial robot factory in Kalamazoo, Michigan in 1989. This was almost the end of the great American robot era. The Americans had been good at inventing but could not change with the times when the market had matured and new technology was made available.

Several American robot manufacturers had invested too much in complexity. General Electric for example, who ran its own robot enterprise for a time, started with a four-arm robot that was to carry out several assembly jobs simultaneously. The problem was that the robot was so complicated it often broke down. The Japanese and Europeans proved to be better at keeping it simple. For example, the Japanese robots contained, on average, 30 percent fewer parts than the American ones.

Another difference was that the American engineers working on the development of industrial robots generally had very little practical experience of factory work. Even at management level, there was a large difference in this area. Companies in the USA were generally run by businessmen while it was often engineers controlling the Japanese robot companies.

At least the company Adept Technology arose from the remains of Unimation. Behind the company were two former workers from Unimation, Bruce Shimano and Brian Carlisle. They did not think Westinghouse were investing enough in development and started producing SCARA indust-

American businesses were generally run by businessmen, whereas engineers often controlled the Japanese robot companies.

rial robots at a factory in San Jose, California. Remaining "in the field of play" was also Cincinnati Milacron, whose concept was still watertight.

General Motors and Fanuc

General Motors became tired of the slow rate of development within the American robotics industry in the beginning of the 1980s and decided to enter the industry themselves. They did so in 1982, in collaboration with the Japanese company Fanuc. Before the joint venture company GM Fanuc was established, GM had first looked into the possibility of co-operating with eight different American companies. None of these, however, were willing to take the risk of being swallowed up by GM. Fanuc took the chance willingly, as this type of company set-up was very common in Japan.

Swedish investment in Japan

Asea invested heavily to establish themselves on the Japanese market. In 1982, they opened an Asea Robot Center in Kobe. A production unit was also planned in Kobe, which was to produce 1,000 robots a year, while a sales office for robot systems was established in Tokyo. The enterprise was run as a new robot division within Gadelius, a company in the Asea owned Fläkt group.

Their intention was to become one of the largest suppliers of advanced

CHAPTER 7
New owners and new partners

robot systems to Japanese industry but they soon found themselves in a real hornets' nest as Japan already produced over 20,000 robots per year. Six robots were sold during their first year of operations, the first one beeing used for lost vax handling of turbine blades. Two years later, they were up to a volume of 160 robots. Although it was not a question of large volumes, Asea Robotics was the market leader in Japan for robots used for deburring, grinding and casting.

Close contact

Asea tried to keep close contact between Sweden and Japan and at least one Japanese was always present at their training courses in Västerås. However, things went very slowly. Japan is one of the toughest markets for foreign newcomers and to have any chance at all, you must prove you are more than twice as good as the domestic companies. It is no coincidence that several large Japanese car manufacturers chose to work with one robot manufacturer for a long period, which was advantageous to both parties, of course. This way of working is a form of long term relationship found between the buyer and seller in different areas of industry throughout Japan.

An expensive lesson

In 1987, Asea decided to move their production back to Sweden. It was just not possible for them to compete in the cut-throat price war as the Japanese manufacturers often sold industrial robots at much lower prices than Asea.

Another problem that Asea experienced with the robot market in Japan was that the competition introduced new models every year, while Asea held on to their "pet" models. The Japanese robot manufacturers of today are trying to distance themselves from this model hysteria and standardise components as much as possible. In the 1980s, however, there was a lot of prestige in being able to offer many variations.

New strategy

Shame on those who give up. After Asea's merger with the Swiss company Brown Boveri in 1988, which resulted in a change of name to ABB, they decided to change strategy and signed a distribution agreement with one of Japan's leading electronics companies, Matsushita Electric.

However, their agreement held for only a few years and ABB then chose to contin-

Japanese Matsushita, with whom ABB signed a distribution agreement, manufactured small assembly robots themselves.

Cincinnati Milacron were specialists in robots for spot welding. ABB Robotics acquired the Cincinnati Milacron robot division in 1990.

ue on their own. Today, ABB, together with Adept, is the only non-Japanese robot manufacturer that is active on the Japanese market.

A similar agreement to the one with Matsushita was signed between ABB and Samsung Heavy Industry for the South Korean market. Samsung were in great need of automation and stood for a large share of the robot acquisitions.

Sought volume benefits

By the end of the 1980s, most manufacturers with an annual production volume below 1,000 robots had to start looking for a partner. At least this volume was required to be able to earn back the development costs for a new robot model. Large companies buying up small, specialised companies was a growing trend.

In 1990, ABB Robotics acquired Cincinnati Milacron's robot division. Cincinnati mainly supplied equipment for spot-welding to the automotive industry. Their robot division had 200 employees and they ran their operations in Greenwood, South Carolina. In connection with the acquisition, the division was moved to the ABB plants in New Berlin and Rochester Hill. Seventy or so employees followed and, together with ABB's previous USA resources, they created an efficient service team. ABB Robotics increased their share of the USA market considerably through the acquisition and gained a share of the attractive market for the after sales service of

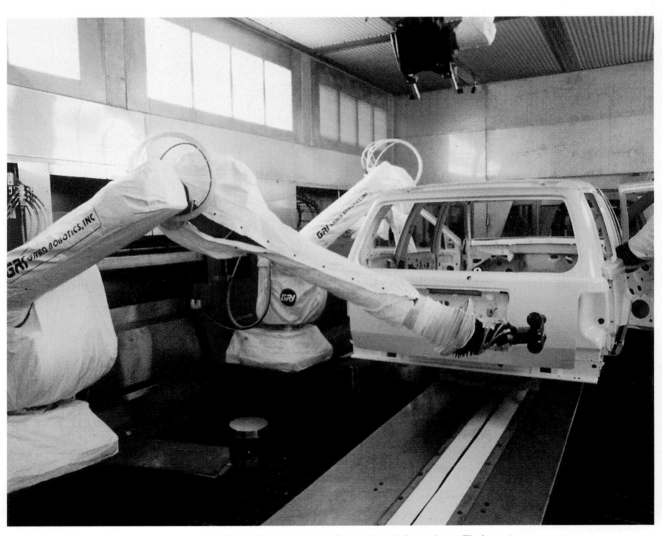

Graco Robotics manufactured painting robots. Their customers were mainly in the automotive industry and its sub-contractors

When ABB Robotics acquired Esab Robotics in 1992, their competitiveness in the arc-welding market increased. Esab had installed around 5000 welding robots worldwide over the years.

robots that Cincinnati Milacron had installed. They aimed to become as big as GM-Fanuc on the American market and saw great potential in America as only half as many robots were installed there compared to Europe.

Strong position in robotised painting

The same kind of tactics was employed when, in 1991, ABB acquired the American Company Graco Robotics located in Plymouth, outside Detroit, who manufactured painting robots. This company was started in 1981 and had about one hundred employees. Graco had installed around 700 robots for painting in North America and South Korea. Their customers came mainly from the automotive industry and its subcontractors. By amalgamating the expertise in Graco and Trallfa, they could offer the market a wider choice of painting robots and painting systems. Due to Graco's strong position in South Korea, ABB were able to start a new Robot Automation Center in Seoul. The new company, ABB Graco Robotics, gained a strong position in the area of robotised painting in North America and Korea.

In 1992, ABB Robotics also bought the resources for arc welding that existed in the Swedish company Esab Robotics. Over the years, Esab had installed about 5,000 welding robots around the world and their turnover was approximately 425 million Swedish crowns. The acquisition meant that Esab's robotics operations in Europe and USA were to be integrated in ABB Robotics' local organisations.

At this point in time, arc welding was responsible for approximately 40% of the world's growing robot market.

Concentration of manufacturing

In 1992, ABB Robotics concentrated all manufacturing of industrial robots for their factory in Västerås and the production of painting robots to Trallfa in Bryne, Norway. Among other things, this meant that the production started in Spain in 1982 was concluded.

The reason Asea started manufacturing in Spain at all was because it was the only way to get on the market, considering the high import duties. This hurdle was gradually being lifted, which meant that assembly could be brought home. This was one more step towards gaining large-scale benefits in production. ABB also had production facilities in USA and France in the early 1980s.

ABB buys ACMA

In 1993, ABB bought the company Préciflex Systems, who manufactured tailor-made robot systems for the automotive industry, which was now demanding system solutions; they did not want to buy robots from one supplier and automation systems from another.

ABB also bought Renault Automation's robot company ACMA. This company, which sold between three and four hundred industrial robots per year, had experienced problems with the order intake and did not really keep up with the trend when the prices of robots fell by about 30% during the last few years.

In France, ABB Préciflex Systems became a "Center of Excellence", where there was to be specialist knowledge of automated car body assembly systems. In the past, ABB had run similar centres for welding, painting and water-jet cutting.

ABB Body in White

In 1997, ABB Flexible Automation and Volvo Cars started a joint venture for developing and manufacturing complete car body lines, attracting customers from the automotive industry all over the world. ABB Olofström Automation is a global company with operations in Sweden, Canada, USA and Brazil. Since 1998, the company has been fully owned by ABB and is called ABB Body in White.

8 | The Robot's Promised Land

THE DIFFERENCE BETWEEN AN INDUSTRIAL ROBOT and an automaton is that a robot is flexible and can be adapted to different tasks. The automaton, of course, works with great precision but only with one fixed task.

It is not at all easy to define what a robot is. Even those in the trade can get it wrong, as the division between a robot and another type of assembly machine or automatic machine is rather vague.

Furthermore, the definition of a robot differs between Japan and the Western world. In Japan, even certain manually controlled manipulators and simple sequence controlled manipulators are called robots.

IFR's classification

The International Federation of Robotics, IFR was founded in 1987 by industrial robot organisations in 15 countries. The main task of the IFR, which has members from over 20 countries today, is to support research and development of industrial robots in different ways. Among other things, they arrange the International Symposium on Robotics every year.

When the members of the IFR use the definition robot in ISO 8373, they specify it as being an "automatically controlled, reprogrammable multipurpose machine programmable in three or more axes".

IFR's definition of a service robot is: "A robot which operates semi or fully autonomously to perform services useful to the well-being of humans and equipment, excluding manufacturing operations".

CHAPTER 8

The robot's
promised land

According to this definition, an industrial robot can also be counted as a service robot if it has non-manufacturing functions.

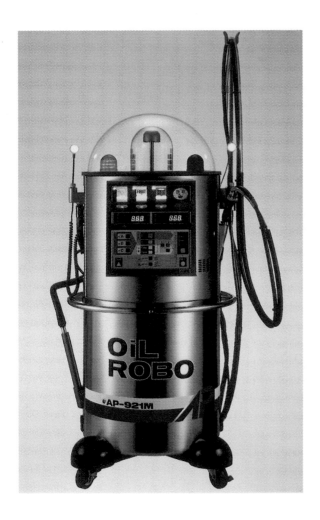

Japanese robot used for changing oil.

An "Eldorado" for robots

Even if the statistics are a little misleading, it is still correct to say that Japan was the robot "Eldorado" of the world. Export shares increased from year to year and the Japanese manufacturers reaped success in both the USA and Europe. The increasingly flourishing countries in Southeast Asia also became an important market for the Japanese.

The European and American competition occasionally commented that the robots installed in Japanese factories were not especially advanced. Nonetheless, the fact remains that they were installed and that productivity was increased.

Support for investment

In 1980, the leasing company, Japan Robot Lease, was started. Their objective

Tax reductions were introduced in 1984 for Japanese companies investing in industrial robots. They were also allowed to borrow money at low interest from national and local authorities.

was to spread robot technology to small and medium sized companies. This company was founded by robot manufacturers Mitsubishi, Fuji and Hitachi and was financed by the state-supported banks Japan Development Bank, Long Term Credit Bank and Industrial Bank of Japan. The company was closed down in 1987, however, due to financial problems.

Tax reductions were introduced in 1984 for companies that invested in Mechatronic Equipment, equipment in which mechanics were integrated with electronics which, of course, is the case with robots. By using this system, the robot user could deduct a further 30% of the value besides the normal deductions. This valuable reform naturally increased interest in the installation of robots in Japan. In addition, companies that wanted to invest could borrow money at low interest rates from the state and local authorities.

Assembly robots

Hitachi was quick off the mark with assembly robots on their production lines. Their first real investment in this area was in the 1970s, in connection with a comprehensive change in the assembly of video tape recorders. Assembly took as much as 35% of the working time. The objective of the project was to reduce the number of assembly workers by 30%, while at the same time increasing productivity by 70%. Those people who became unemployed were retrained to work with software instead, a field

CHAPTER 8
The robot's promised land

in which there was a shortage of personnel. The thought of laying off personnel did not exist in Japan and this was possible due to the continual expansion of the enterprise.

The SCARA robot

In 1981, Sankyo Seiki, Pentel and NEC presented a completely new concept for assembly robots. The robot was developed under the guidance of Hiroshi Makino, a professor at the University of Yamanashi. The robot was called Selective Compliance Assembly Arm, SCARA. Its arm was rigid in the Z-axis and pliable in the XY-axes, which allowed it to adapt to holes in the XY-axes.

Makino considered that approximately 80% of all assembly could be carried out using this type of passive, simple and cheap robot with few axles. When the concept was launched, he maintained that there was a market for one million SCARA robots in Japan alone.

Assembly robots in large numbers

SCARA robots were used for the assembly of both mechanical and electrical products. They were fast and could be seen in large numbers along the assembly lines in Japan.

Approximately 55,000 SCARA and Cartesian robots were being used for assembly work within Japanese industry in 1990. A large number of these were used to fit components onto circuit boards.

Several other Japanese companies also started producing SCARA robots. One of these was Matsushita, who was co-operating with ABB Robotics. They also developed SCARA robot systems for arc welding.

The PUMA assembly robot was manufactured under licence by Kawasaki and the ABB robot IRB 1000 was also used for assembly in Japan.

Two thirds of all robots

Between 1980 and 1988, the number of robots in operation had increased tenfold and in 1988, the figure was 256,000. Of these, 175,000, or 68%, had been installed in Japan.

However, not all Japanese robot manufacturers succeeded completely. Dainichi Kiko, set up in 1971, went bankrupt in 1986. They had been the fastest growing business in the robot industry until one year before the bankruptcy and had a fruitful co-operation with Jaguar Cars in England among others. When the exchange rates for the Japanese Yen went up, Dainichi Kiko could not keep up and several other Japanese manufacturers followed them to the grave.

In 1990, approximately 60,000 robots per year were manufactured in Japan. Of these, about 15,000 were exported. Despite the fact that the number of robots had increased, there was a decrease in the number of robot manufacturers. There were now around 50 companies selling robots in Ja-

One reason for the rapid robotisation in Japan was the great Japanese interest in gadgets. Technicians were forced to think up new products and models to satisfy the discriminating customer.

pan and around 20 manufacturers, of which eight offered a comprehensive range of robots. They were Fanuc, Yaskawa, Kawasaki, Nachi-Fujikoshi, Mitsubishi (Melfa-robot), Toyoda (Friend-robot), Fuji and Matsushita.

Fuji principally made assembly machines for components on circuit boards and loading robots for NC machines.

Mitsubishi Electric used the name Melfa for their robots, while the robots from Mitsubishi Heavy Industries were called Robitus.

There were also Japanese companies that concentrated on making spray-painting robots. Among these were Kobe Steel and Tokico. Kobe Steel first bought licences for spray-painting robots from Trallfa and then started to develop their own.

Left further behind

There were approximately 350,000 robots in operation in Japan in 1991. They had now left the rest of the world even further behind in the robot statistics. Naturally, Japan was the most robot-populated country in the world. In 1992, there were just over 16 robots per 1000 industrial workers, compared to barely eight in Sweden. In the rest of Europe and in the USA the figure was under four.

One reason for the rapid rise in the number of robots was that the Japanese are so fond of new technical gadgets that manufacturers must continually produce new products and models to satisfy the discriminating customer. The consequence of this situation meant that production must be efficient and flexible. This is where the industrial robot also came into the picture within the expansive consumer electronics industry.

The Japanese robot manufacturers bought parts for the robots mainly from domestic suppliers. In the middle of the 1990s, however, the number of foreign components increased. These components were bought largely from Southeast Asia and South America but also from the USA. Certain Japanese manufacturers also moved some of their production to low-income countries and started divisions in the USA and Europe.

Used in final assembly

The car industry in Japan, just as in the rest of the world, is a very large user of industrial robots. They have used robots for spot and arc welding of car bodies since the 1960s. As control and sensor systems were developed, new areas of application were being opened.

Kawasaki was first to commercially launch a 32-bit control system at the end of the 1980s. The servo software gave a high accuracy of movement with up to 14 axles being controlled at the same time. Kobe Steel had a similar system that managed 18 axles at the same time.

The Japanese car manufacturers have been forerunners in developing the assembly line. In the Toyota factories, for example, the final assembly

Flexible Body Line
at one of the Toyota
car factories. The
conveyors are dri-
ven not by chains
but by a type of rol-
ler.

CHAPTER 8
The robot's promised land

consists of a dozen assembly lines that run parallel with each other. The lines are called Flexible Body Line and consist of a conveyor belt driven with a type of roller instead of chains.

Nissan have their own system called Intelligent Body Assembly System, IBAS. This system enables them to produce several models on the same assembly line. Programmable fixtures are then used.

During the 1990s, the Japanese car industry invested heavily in the automation of final assembly. Nissan was one of the companies that made the most headway. In 1993, they introduced robot technology in the final assembly lines in the Zima factory. The robots fitted front seats, wheels, front and rear windows as well as rear lights. One of the robots also filled the brake fluid automatically.

Arc welding

Two trends started to appear in the field of arc welding in the early 1990s. One was the appearance of cheaper and simpler arc welding robots. Matsushita, Daihen and Fanuc were some of the companies that chose to invest in this type of robot.

The other trend was the increased use of joint searching and joint following. When joint following with laser, the laser beam scans the joint before welding. This provides a profile of the joint that the robot can follow.

Spot-welding in the car industry

As regards spot-welding, most of the installations at the beginning of the 1990s took place in the Japanese automotive industry. Spot-welding was being used almost exclusively for the assembly of car bodies in Japan. Kawasaki was the market-leading manufacturer of spot-welding robots and Fanuc and Nachi-Fujikoshi were also industrious manufacturers. Besides these, Yaskawa and Mitsubishi Electric were also on the list of manufacturers.

Fanuc and Nachi used a method called poke welding. It worked in such a way that the robot pressed together the sheets against a fixed back-stop.

Laser systems for welding with robots began to appear early in the 1990s. Amongst other things, they were used in the manufacture of the Toyota Lexus. There were also a number of laser systems for cutting.

Fanuc had developed a robot, on behalf of General Motors, that was suitable for directing laser beams via mirrors. Among other things, it could be used for making holes on finished car bodies.

When it came to machine handling, link arm robots were most common. Fanuc, for example, had several such installations in their own factories.

Designed a program for stacking

Several Japanese robot manufacturers had produced robots for palletisation and handling. One important area of use was handling television tubes, which had become larger and more difficult to handle. This type of robot had to be fast and able to handle large loads.

Advanced AI-programs (artificial intelligence) for palletisation were being produced in the early 1990s. By stating the size and weight of the box, its starting point and the size and position of the pallet, the system could carry out a program for stacking. The program also took into consideration the weight and made sure that the centre of gravity of the load on the pallet was within permitted values.

Inspected the paintwork

An increasing number of robots were needed for inspection and testing. Checking the dimensions in the car body assembly lines, for example, was an important area. Another example was the inspection of painted surfaces on finished cars. Testing and inspection of circuit boards and electronic appliances was also a large field of use in Japan.

Spreading glue and sealant provided another common area of use for robots. Fanuc, Nachi and Kawasaki produced a robot for sealing welded joints on car bodies that had tubes inside the upper arm so that it was possible to transport sealant to the pistol.

One example of a gluing application was fitting windscreens and rear windows in cars. Ever since the end of the 1980s, these had been fitted using glue that was spread using a certain type of robot.

Robot programming language

In the early 1990s, the International Standards Organisation, ISO, was working to standardise robot programming. The programming language for man-machine communication is known as user language. In addition, there is machine code for the control program, i.e. machine-machine communication.

An important requirement for user language is that it can be used interactively. There were two schools of thought for the structure of the user language. One was that the language should be simple and able to be used by the operators themselves without comprehensive computer training. The other was that the language should fulfil sophisticated computer requirements and that only specially trained technicians should be allowed to perform the programming. An example of the first philosophy was ABB's robot language ARLA. Fanuc's robot language KAREL is an example of the second.

The Japanese preferred to use the simpler robot language, while in the USA there were advocates for the more advanced language. This led, for example, to manufacturers wanting to work worldwide often having to use two programming languages.

Size does matter

A trend in Japanese robot manufacturing during the 1990s has been to approach small and medium-sized companies, who have increased their interest in investing in robot technology, to a greater extent than earlier.

Another trend is to develop smaller robots. This is because, as a rule, there is too little space in the Japanese factories. The size of the robot, therefore, has been significant in the management's decision regarding investment.

Developing robot systems with several external axles working synchronously with each other is another 1990s phenomenon.

Mass-production was once the most important thing in Japan. Now it is more user-friendly.

Previously in Japan, mass-production and mass sales had been most important. Nowadays, they invest many more working hours on creating user-friendly products.

Technology centre in Tokyo

In 1994, JARA opened a new technology centre, the Robot Simulation Centre, in Tokyo. This meeting place was aimed at raising the level of knowledge regarding robot technology, developing new technology for the adaptation of robot installations and increasing the use of robots within the manufacturing industry. Computerised robot simulating systems were installed in the centre. At the centre, specialists could help with the layout work for robot installations and calculate cycle times and production costs. Those customers interested in the installation of robots were able to hire robot simulation equipment from the centre.

Japanese robot manufacturers were also deeply involved in the Ecofactory project run by the AIST (Agency of Industrial Science and Technology). The purpose of this project was to develop next generation technology that would contribute to decreasing environmental pollution without sacrificing profitability or technical development within the manufacturing industry.

In practice, this meant developing multi-axis robots and intelligent control systems and sensors that enabled the robot to identify different structures, materials and the method of dismantling parts.

Robots for all areas

The Japanese have been very keen to develop types of robots other than

Fanuc introduced their "intelligent" robot I-211 in 1999. It could be used to automate even the most demanding assembly processes.

just industrial robots. There are many examples from the 1990s of tests with mobile robots that walked or rolled around. Takaoka Electric constructed a device that managed 18-centimetre high steps and loads of up to 100 kilos on a 40-degree inclination. It went up stairs at a speed of two kilometres an hour.

Fanuc's new intelligent robots

During the 1999 International Robot & Vision Show in Detroit, Fanuc presented an entirely new kind of "intelligent robot" – the I-211. With this robot, it should be possible to automate even the most demanding assembly processes. The robot has been equipped with a 3D-image sensor and a 6-axes power sensor. It can pick up things that are spread out on an assembly belt, which means there is no need to invest in feed equipment to the same extent as earlier.

The I-211 was originally produced for assembling mini-robots in Fanuc's own factory.

9 | ABB Leads Technical Development

When Asea introduced the IRB 6, they first had to convince the market that there was a real need for industrial robots. Industry in the West was not fully prepared to accept robots and Asea, together with other robot manufacturers, were forced to put a lot of effort into developing applications. This showed results and the success reported by some customers awoke the curiosity of others that had chosen to wait and see.

Product development accelerated in the early 1980s. One important break-through was the introduction of the "seeing" robot from Unimation. In 1983, Asea Robotics produced its first seeing robot, IRB 90. The image processing system electronics and software were now integrated. The factory workers themselves could carry out the programming and program revisions. Broadly speaking, this consisted of teaching the system to recognise the objects that the robot was to handle. The operator placed the part under one of the system cameras and a contour appeared on the screen that the operator then marked and transferred to the computer memory. The system, which could be applied to any robot, could remember up to 99 objects and recognised a workpiece in many different positions. The computer informed the robot, which could then check or grip the object.

A unique control lever

Asea's first seeing robot was installed at Asea Control in Västerås, whe-

The IRB 6 was the subject for a Swedish postage stamp in 1984.

Product development at Asea Robotics really took off in the early 1980s. IRB 90 was a specially designed robot for spot welding that could also be used for handling materials.

re it was part of the production line for contactors. The robot picked up plastic parts from a conveyor belt and made sure they were processed in a machine group.

IRB 90 was especially suited to spot-welding and could be used for handling materials. The new control system, S2, made it possible to control several axles and, in addition, Asea had developed a unique control lever.

Thanks to the new control system, more and more users were able to program the robot. The programming was carried out in the language of their choice and the program capacity was multiplied. Robots were now being seriously included at the assembly stage.

The world's fastest robot

In 1984, Asea produced the world's fastest assembly robot, the IRB 1000. This was an innovative concept in that it was equipped with a vertical arm, a sort of hanging "pendulum robot". This meant that the robot could work quickly across a large area without the need to traverse. The robot boasted high acceleration values, 2G, an advantage in assembly work involving short distances. It was as much as 50% faster than conventional arm robots.

The advantage of the IRB 1000 compared with the Japanese SCARA robots was the greater degree of freedom. The IRB 1000 was rewarded with the Leonardo da Vinci award.

Asea Robotics' robot workshop, Jonas, in 1986. Here, industrial robots are assembled. In the foreground are IRB 90 robots being tested.

The largest robot factory

The Swedish export minister, Mats Hellström, opened a new robot factory in Västerås in 1985. The 300 metre long factory, with its 13,000 square metres, is one of the largest factories in the world.

Asea Robotics had grown out of its old factory. The company was going well, they had 1,500 employees and a turnover of just over one billion Swedish crowns. In the last few years, their sales had increased by 50% each year, while the world market for robots had increased by approximately 25% per year. The annual capacity in the new factory was initially about 1,200 robots.

ABB's investment in the robot factory was based on an optimistic prognosis in the industry. They saw the automotive industry making large investments while, at the same time, industrialists, politicians and researchers were promoting robots as the key technology for the future.

Divided into product workshops

The factory was divided into a number of product workshops that, with its small range of products, was able to ensure fast delivery to the customers. Besides fully-fledged robot systems, they also delivered semi-manufactured products in large numbers to Asea Robotics' other production plants in the USA, Japan, France and Spain.

During the opening ceremony of the factory, they took the opportunity of presenting the new welding robot, IRB 9000S, which was also a robot of pendulum type. The IRB 9000S was principally intended for use in the automotive industry. Its arrival made it possible to use more robots per workstation than before and perform spot-welding that floor standing robots could not manage. The model was based largely on the IRB 90.

One important factor in the choice of spot-welding robots is that they must be fast and manage as many welds as possible per cycle. For spot-welding, the robot must be able to manage 60–70 kilos and often 100 kilos in the automotive industry.

The use of coated sheet metal increased to obtain a somewhat improved rust-protection. This put much greater demands on the welding process.

Time for alternating current

The IRB 2000 arc-welding robot was launched in 1986. It evolved from an egg at a trade fair in Brussels. It was important to take advantage of all the publicity you could get to attract attention. The IRB 2000 was run by the S3 control system, the first time alternating current was used to operate the motors on an ABB robot. AC motors offered better cooling, which meant that improved performance could be obtained. This shift in technology took place around the same time for all manufacturers of industrial robots.

The IRB 1000 was the fastest assembly robot in the world. The innovation with this concept was that it was equipped with a vertical arm, a type of suspended "pendulum robot". This IRB 1000 is being used for manufacturing shoes.

In 1987, Asea Robotics increased their range of products by also developing a robot with a folding arm, the "Asea High Speed SCARA", designated IRB 300. This robot was intended for handling small components.

During the latter part of the 1980s, the robot industry made a technical advancement when it began using vision to identify and determine the position of an object to a greater extent than previously, using laser scanners for measuring welded joints for arc welding and force sensors for grinding, burring and casting. ABB Robotics introduced the LaserTrak sensor for this purpose in 1986.

Simpler and cheaper

ABB Robotics dominated the European market in 1990, while GM Fanuc was largest in the USA. ABB was considered more advanced in user-friendliness and in systems approach, while the Japanese were very good at adapting to the requirements of the customer.

The IRB 2000 arc-welding robot evolved from an egg at the show in Brussels.
It was the first AC-powered Asea robot. The AC motor offered better cooling,
which meant that it could deliver a higher performance.

The demand for robots, however, was not as great as many people had predicted in the 1970s. The failure of the boom to arrive was probably not principally due to the inferior technical advancement of the robots. A more important probable cause was that it took too long to reprogram them. In the pursuit of more features, the designers sometimes forget that the robot must be easy for the operators to use.

If a product is correctly designed from the start, it makes it much easier to introduce new robot technology. If the product is difficult to assemble manually, it will be even harder for a robot.

The robots of the 1990s would prove to be simpler, cheaper and easier to install and use. Most of the development, therefore, took place on the software side of things.

A new spot-welding robot

Most industrial robots were still being used for spot-welding. Several successful companies were already in the market and at ABB, they had also started to consider whether to introduce a spot-welding robot. However, this was no easy decision. Stelio Demark, who had taken over as MD after Björn Weichbrodt in 1987, and the members of his team were wiping sweat from their brows before the important decision was made to profile the company as a manufacturer of spot-welding robots.

The IRB 6000 was launched in 1991 and it became ABB's first success-

ful spot-welding robot. It was a large robot, which could handle 150 kilos and this signified a great breakthrough in the car industry. The IRB 6000 was mainly used for spot-welding and handling materials and was produced in close collaboration with customers, who were involved from the appearance of the very first drawing. Its modular concept meant it could be easily adapted to many different applications.

It could be said that it was a tailor-made robot with the advantages of a standard product. The robot was composed of modules and had 60% fewer parts than its predecessor, the IRB 90. It was produced to meet the price cuts that the Japanese manufacturers, in particular, were employing. The IRB 6000 could be utilised for many different needs.

Water-jet cutting

Punching with warm knives can cause toxic gases and manual cutting easily causes stress injuries. Both these problems were eliminated with the introduction of water-jet cutting, which became all the more popular during the 1990s. It is an environment-friendly method, which works on the principal of water under high pressure producing a cutting jet. Technically, it is comparatively simple. Water is pressurised until it reaches 3,000 bar, then it passes through a hole in a diamond or sapphire, after which the jet of water attains a speed of two to three times the speed of sound. Then, it is simply a matter of cutting, using a robot to automate the process. It ta-

IRB 6000 became ABB Robotics' most successful spot-welding robot. It was their first modular robot model, in that the upper arm could have different lengths and the "wrist" different dimensions. In other words, a tailor made robot with the advantages of a standard robot.

ABB I-R are specialists in water-jet cutting and world-leaders in advanced 3D water-jet cutting systems.

kes about 40 hours to complete an entirely new program, but variations need only simple additions or revisions, which take, at most, eight hours.

Fine cut

Among the advantages of water-jet cutting is that the cut is very fine, thanks to the small diameter of the nozzle and that the material is not heated or exposed to forces when cut, for example with a saw.

Some of the materials that could be cut in this way were paper, plastic, foodstuffs, rubber and glass. Within the automotive industry, they cut roof interiors, carpets, interior panels for doors and instrument panels.

This unique cutting system was developed by ABB I-R Waterjet Systems, who had their head office in Ronneby. This company was started in 1991 as a spin-off from the company Best Matic, who had been working with this process since 1974. ABB I-R is specialised in waterjet cutting and a world leader in advanced three-dimensional water jet-cutting systems.

Pioneering control system

The merging of ABB Robotics with Esab Robotics in 1992 resulted in the robot IRB 1500, which was intended mainly for arc welding. It replaced the IRB 6, which had been discontinued the year before. The new welding robot was compared to a "helper", a person that had earlier assisted the skilled welders. In this way, the welders could concentrate on the job in hand.

With the S4 control system, robot performance was greatly improved with regard to accuracy and cycle time. The robot control system could now control six internal axes, all the welding parameters and up to six external axes. The robot was controlled by very powerful microprocessors. Within ABB, some regard the development of the S4 control system as being as big a step as Asea's introduction of their first industrial robot.

The fusion between ABB Robotics and Esab
Robotics resulted in new, advanced arc-welding
robots. The IRB 2000, with its prize-winning
design, was the most popular arc-welding robot
for many years.

CHAPTER 9

*ABB leads
technical
development*

Compared to the IRB 6, the computing capacity of the microprocessor had increased one thousand-fold.

At the beginning of the 1990s, the robotics industry found themselves in a similar position to the computer industry of the 1960s, when the potential of technology was limited by deficient programming and system construction.

An open system

The S4 control system took a total of 150 man-years to develop. Now it was time for the robot's "muscles" to be utilised to the full and the "brain" no longer hindered "the body's" ability to work quickly and precisely. One important advantage was that new robot systems could be integrated with other automation equipment. They had created an open control system that was able to communicate with other systems nearby and did not just communicate between themselves as the old control systems did.

Drop-down menus and dialog boxes

The S4 was programmed using the same technology that was used when working with personal computers, with drop down menus and dialog boxes for example. This was a revolution within the robot industry and programming was now much easier. This system was chosen because, among other reasons, the younger automation technicians were already

used to working with personal computers. Now they were able to program their robot without even needing access to a real robot station and could even do this sitting at home on the sofa.

The total cycle time for robots was reduced by up to 35% and the accuracy of repeatability was improved by approximately ten times. The reduced cycle time meant that the production capacity could be greatly increased. The increase in the accuracy of repeatability gave a more consistent and higher quality. This resulted in selling the robot to industries where the demand for accuracy in movement was essential.

Aggressive pricing

Through aggressive pricing, ABB Robotics tried to reach a large market among customers that were buying automatic welding systems for the first time. There were great problems in co-ordinating deliveries for the competition in this area of the market, who bought robots from Japan, welding equipment from the USA and other equipment from local suppliers. This was the most customer-adapted product that ABB had so far produced and they recognised the potential with small and medium-sized companies that had problems recruiting skilled welders.

Reduced pay-off time

The pay-off time for the investment in robots was continually reduced during the early 1990s and, generally, it was somewhere between one and two years. This was due to robots accomplishing more for the invested capital, compared to skilled workers who demanded high wages.

ABB companies produced 3,000 robots in 1993, the same amount that had existed in the whole world ten years earlier. Half the ABB robots were sold to the automotive industry, where they were mainly used for welding and spray painting and where the demand for precision and function was extremely high.

Largest order ever

In 1993, ABB Robotics signed an agreement with General Motors of Europe for the sale of 500 industrial robots. It was the company's largest single order ever.

General Motors was generally very interested in the robot automation of their factories. In some cases, however, their visions went a little too far and they were forced to close down their factory of the future, the Vanguard Plant in Saginaw, Michigan, in 1994. It was here that General Motors intended to manufacture components in a "lights-out-factory", a computer-controlled unmanned factory, where not even lights were needed. However, the control system became so complicated that in the end, it was impossible to maintain.

Ford was also a big customer of ABB's. For Ford's new "Car for the World", the Mondeo, the robot became an important part in the process.

Painting robots

After the fusion between Asea Robotics and Trallfa in 1985, Trallfa chose to switch from hydraulic to electric control. The conversion went off with hardly any hitches and this technical approach towards the IRB robots gave them added clout in the market.

Trallfa had produced the painting robot TR 510 in 1992, the first of its kind to use fibre optics in its control system.

In 1994, they signed an agreement with the Low Emission Paint Consortium, LEPC, concerning a collaboration with Chrysler, Ford and General Motors, on the design and installation of a test plant where new painting techniques for the car industry could be developed.

TRACS, Trallfa Robot Automotive Coating System, was a fully integrated system concept developed for spray painting cars. Besides painting robots, the system also included manipulators for opening doors, bonnets and boots. To open doors is one of the most complicated stages in a fully automatic spray painting system. It is often necessary to have the door or boot lid in more than one position

All the functions in a TRACS system were controlled from a central computer and reprogramming could be performed off-line. Automatic spray painting is process technology at a high level and includes everything from colour systems and programming to quality of the finished product.

ABB developed a whole family of software products that went under the name Paintware at their plant in Bryne, Norway. They also had the car painting system, to be known as FlexPainter, under development. Many solutions were based on the IRB 5400 robot, which was built on the same principal as all the other ABB robots.

Into the food industry

In the late 1990s, robot automation proved that it could contribute to solving the dilemma in which the European consumer goods industry found itself. On the one hand, production was being concentrated on much larger factories that produced enormous volumes. On the other

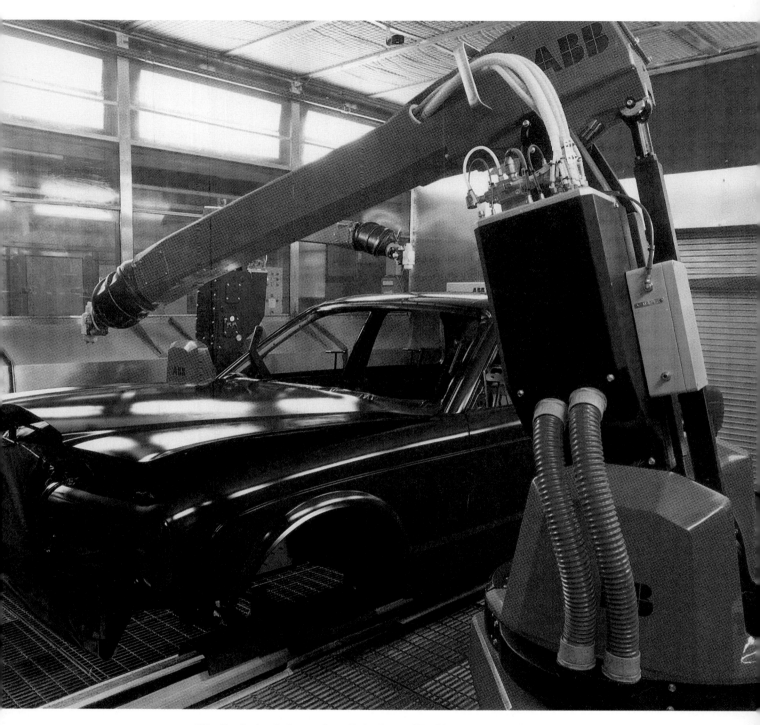

After the fusion between Asea Robotics and Trallfa in 1985, Trallfa chose to switch from a hydraulic to an electric control system. The conversion went off with hardly any hitches. The TR 5000 painting robot is used mainly in the automotive industry.

hand, the demand for market adjustment increased at the same rate as the market grew and new products were introduced. The only solution was flexible production with greater demand for availability and flexibility in the machine park that handled and produced the products.

Apart from robots making it possible to achieve improved ergonomics on packing lines, they could also be used for picking, packaging and palletisation of vessels and boxes. The technology could be used for handling products such as coffee, ice cream and dairy products just as well as beverages and chocolate.

Packaging of champagne bottles

One example that ABB Robotics proudly refers to is the French producer of champagne, Mumm, who have used robots in their packing lines ever since 1979. The result has been a faster flow in production, fewer rejects and a reduced need of space. Nowadays, most of the French champagne manufacturers are using robots.

Another reference is the results that were achieved at the chocolate manufacturers, Milka, in Switzerland, who replaced conventional packing machines with robots. Milka use five robots for placing a various number of chocolate bars of different sizes in three different boxes. Earlier, these were counted manually at six packing lines.

The same robots also pack the chocolate. Each robot handles 31 tons of chocolate per shift, which, according to Milka, results in greater production speed and a better working environment. The robots can easily be reset for different types of packages and be used for quality control of the chocolate bar wrappers as well.

The industrial robot fulfils the high demands of the consumer goods industry on productivity and it can be used for a wide spectrum of products, while the short resetting time allows for a high degree of utilisation.

FlexPalletizer

In 1997, ABB Robotics developed a model called the FlexPalletizer designed for palletisation. This monotonous and strenuous job is well suited to a machine and, in many cases, a robot is a better solution than a traditional pallet loader, especially in confined spaces and when there are demands on flexibility, e.g. when different articles to the same customer are to be loaded on to the same pallet. There are already many robots for such functions in Europe.

The fastest picking robot

In 1998, ABB Robotics developed the world's fastest picking robot, FlexPicker, which was able to pick 120 objects a minute. It accelerated with 10 G and could pick and release at a speed of 10 metres per second, using image technology. ABB now had a picking robot just as versatile as a human manual worker, able to handle a wide range of small items, from electronic components to pieces of chocolate. This meant that application in new areas of industry, such as the food industry for example, was now possible.

The origin of the FlexPicker was the Delta robot developed by Professor Reymond Clavel at EPFL in Switzerland.

Wash Down

Project FlexPicker WD, where WD stood for "Wash Down", began in 1999. Within the food industry, especially in the area of exposed food, hygiene is of extreme importance. Demands on the robot were that it should cope with washing processes and be easy to clean. They aimed at making the manipulator as tight as possible and improving the seals and panels. Stainless steel would have been the best material to cope with the aggressive detergents. However, this could not be used because the weight of the moving parts would be too great. As ABB's entire concept for the FlexPicker was built on reducing the weight of these parts, they produced a new arm system in aluminium instead that was surface treated by hard anodising. Hard anodising gives an incredibly hard and resistant surface. Thanks to this, a special version of the washdown FlexPicker could be created.

FlexPicker, introduced in 1998, was the fastest picking robot in the world. It accelerates with 10 G and can pick and release at a speed of 10 metres per second.

Automation in foundries

The customers of today demand lighter and more efficient cars, which has lead to the increase in the use of aluminium parts. Automation of large casting machines is a must for those who want to be a part of this progress.

Casting is a very suitable job for a robot. The working conditions are among the worst to be found in the manufacturing industry. The operator is exposed to high temperatures while he prepares the next casting with the machine open. The machine must not be open for very long, which puts pressure on the operator. A robot in this case may not work faster than the operator but, in the long run, the robot is more efficient because it does not need to take any breaks and it can withstand heat.

ABB has produced a complete automation solution for casting, containing a number of production cells for all stages of the casting process.

Automation of the entire process

As regards the automotive industry, ABB is investing in a higher degree of automation for the entire process, from the assembly of ready-made parts to the finished car body. By using standardised units, it is possible to construct a complete robot line for car manufacturing, from supplying the presses to the finished, unpainted car. Such types of complete plants have been delivered to car manufacturers in Europe.

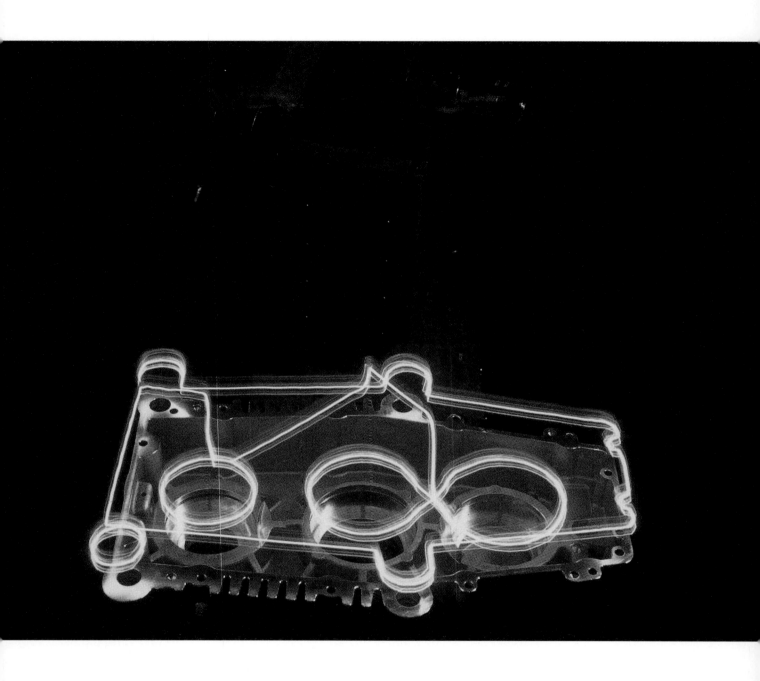

Foundries are a very favourable field for robots as the working conditions must be amongst the worst in the manufacturing industry. Shown here are castings being deburred.

It is also important to reduce the cycle times in the factory. At Segerström & Svensson in Eskilstuna, a large subcontractor to the Swedish car industry, an unusual variation of robot stations is used in production. In double stations, two ABB robots share welding equipment, welding positioner and fixtures. Two common stations have been combined together to become one, which means the user gains both space and time. In this case, there is no need to buy a fixture for each robot, since they share a mutual welding positioner. By having double robots, a 60–70% higher capacity is obtained when welding large series. The surface area where a guard rail is necessary can also be reduced. Segerström & Svensson are today using four double stations.

Co-operating with the customer

Robots and control cabinets are assembled in ABB's robot workshop with subcontractors, most of them in Europe, supplying all the components. The use of robots in production is becoming more common even with the subcontractors in order assure quality. To be able to meet market demands, ABB has invested in "core technology".

The hardest stage in selling industrial robots is convincing potential customers that robots are a good and sound financial investment. It is, therefore, very important to understand what the real needs of the customer are.

Continual improvements

The general trend in the robot market is characterised by tight changes of generation and price cuts. This is why continual improvements that will lead to more efficient working methods and cost reductions are part of the normal working day. Thanks to this, the development time for new robots during the last few years has been halved, new robot systems contain fewer components which means shorter assembly times than their predecessors and the trial periods have been greatly reduced.

Quality system

ABB Robotics' quality system was ISO 9001 certified in 1992. In 1997, they obtained their ISO 14001 certificate and in 1998, ABB Robotics became the first in Europe to meet the requirements for the car industry standard QS 9000/TE Supplement. QS is a branch interpretation of ISO 9000, which was established by The Big Three, i.e. Chrysler, Ford and General Motors in the USA. QS is short for Quality System Requirements, TE is short for Tooling Equipment and deals with demands on the quality system for the supply of tools and equipment. This standard is sure to become all the more significant within the industry, partly because it is being applied in several different segments of industry.

One of the deciding factors when choosing a robot supplier is, of course, trust in the product. The customer knows that a supplier who is com-

pliant with QS 9000/TE Supplement will work in a methodical way to develop and manufacture a functionally reliable product.

Self confidence

Stelio Demark, MD for ABB Robotics until 1999, sums up the 1990s as a maturing and consolidating phase for the company. It has developed from an entrepreneur-oriented organization to a company also taking financial responsibility.

Product development has principally revolved around efficiency and reliability.

What Demark is actually saying is that, during its first 25 years, ABB Robotics built up a self-confidence that is now the foundation on which they can base their bold targets for the 21st century.

THE GOLDEN ROBOT AWARD

The Golden Robot Award, initially known as the Asea Robot Award, was presented for the first time in 1984. The purpose of the award is to stimulate research and development of industrial robots. The Golden Robot Award consists of a gold plated IRB 6 mounted on a block of masur birch as well as a diploma. It is awarded annually at the ISR.

Winners of the award:
1984 Wilhelm Kirch, Ford Motor, Germany.
1985 Hiroshi Makino, Yamanashi University, Japan.
1986 Rolf D. Schraft, IPA, Germany
1987 Hendrik Van Brussel, Leuven Katholieke University, Belgium.
1988 Stig Sandström, Best Matic, Sweden.
1989 John F. Hinrichs, A.O. Smith Automotive Products, USA.
1990 Yokio Hasegawa, Waseda University, Japan.
1991 Geary V. Soska, Goodyear Tire & Rubber, USA.
1992 Carl Erik Skjoelstrup, Odense Steel Shipyard, Denmark.
1993 Kanji Yonemoto, JIRA, Japan.
1994 Bernhard Bula, Bula & Fils, Switzerland.
1995 Egon Olszewski, Benteler, Germany.
1996 François Ronssin, Philips Display Components, France.
1997 Jong-Oh Park, Korea Institute of Science and Technology, South Korea.
1998 Hisanori Nakamura, Toyota Motor, Japan.
1999 Reymond Clavel, EPFL, Switzerland
    Karl-Erik Neumann, Neos Robotics, Sweden

A FEW OTHER INNOVATORS IN THE ROBOT FIELD

Fast growing manufacturer

The American robot manufacturer, Adept Technology, was started in 1983 and has grown rapidly. Today, the company has about 400 employees. At the time when Adept was founded, there were around 50 robot manufacturers in the USA. Today, they are the only ones left on that continent.

Adept has supplied about 15,000 robot systems worldwide and the assembly robot "AdeptOne" has become a huge success. V+robot Language and its follow up VAL is the world's most advanced software for robots.

Camau's pre-twisted cables

Comau's new industrial robot "Smart H4" has solved the problem of hanging cables. All the cables in the Smart H4 are run inside the robot all the way to the wrist. The heat generated in slip rings during welding can cause troublesome condensation. This design means that the problems sometimes arising when normal slip rings are used can be avoided.

Comau was inspired by the aircraft industry, which used pre-twisted cables. They found this technical solution at a small robotics company called Bisiach & Carru in Turin.

The Tricept robot is a type of combination of a robot and a processing machine. Here, the Tricept 805 is employed with processing floor beams at Boeing, Wichita.

The robot that stood firm

The innovator Karl Erik Neumann, who started the company Neos Robotics in Täby, presented the robot Tricept for the first time in 1994 at Comau's stand at the Hannover show. It is an entirely new type of robot, a type of combination of a robot and a processing machine.

The machine sits with its three arms in a three-legged stand, which means that it is more stable than conventional industrial robots and more flexible than numerically controlled machines.

HARRY SORTS THE BOOKS

There are many ways to use a robot. At the town library in Örnsköldsvik in Sweden in 1994, they installed the first robot in the world to facilitate the handling of returned books. The robot was christened Harry.

The system worked so that the borrower of the book placed one book at a time on a belt. A scanner read the bar code on the back of the book and the robot then picked the book from the belt and placed it in a basket. A lifting arm lifted up the basket when it was full and put it on a book trolley. After this, the librarian took the trolley and placed the books on their respective shelves.

The primary purpose of Harry, which is an ABB robot, was to give the employees a better working environment. Occupational hazards for many librarians are injuries to elbows, wrists, shoulders and neck as they twist and turn repeatedly in their daily handling of books. By increasing and improving the level of service at the library, personnel were free to help the borrowers.

Harry is no longer in commission but the library in Malmö does have a similar system.

10 | A Bright Future for the Robot

THE NUMBER OF INDUSTRIAL ROBOTS installed rose considerably during the nineties. In 1992, there were 466,000 robots in operation and 720,000 in 1998, an increase of 54 percent.

What does the future hold for the industrial robot? In reality, it has so far only reached any volume in the field of spot-welding. However, volume is also increasing relatively quickly in areas such as arc welding, assembly, die-casting, packing and painting.

Today, industrial robots are employed in roughly 20 different fields and a recent study carried out by ABB showed that there are around 900 potential fields of use in the future.

One can be so bold as to say that robot automation is still in its initial stages. We could have a "revolution" ahead of us. Could we be talking about a full invasion of more than 100,000 robot installations each year or...? Much of this depends on the robot manufacturers being able to package the software more effectively. The robots of the future will probably be much more self-contained than they are today. Better sensors must be made to support these robots if such a development is to take place. Robot designers were already imitating human senses when they developed robot sensors. The time taken to programme a robot must also be speeded up. At present, it can take many hours to program a robot to do what a welder can be instructed to do in one minute.

Much has happened even in this area during the nineties. As the IT fi-

CHAPTER 10
*A bright future
for the robot*

eld matured, the interest of the robot manufacturers in information technology also increased and the communication between man, PC and robot was improved.

Another step forward in technology that is on the threshold is a control system that can control much more than just the robot. It will have control over almost all the peripheral activities.

Furthermore, it will be necessary to establish a common robot programming language. This would be a very positive contribution to development.

Prices for industrial robots dropped by 30–50% in USA, Germany, France and Great Britain between 1989 and 1999. The pay-off time for a robot installation has been almost halved during the same period. The price war will become all the tougher and when prices do fall, the customer's desire for robot automation will increase. Today, it is even possible to sell robots to low income countries. The strength of the robot is its ability to perform a job to the same standard of quality throughout. This is of course essential in countries with cheap labour.

1997 was the best year regarding the number of robot installations so far, with 85,000 robots being sold that year. This figure dropped to 71,000 in 1998, mainly due to a drop in sales in Japan and South Korea. Discounting these two countries, the number of installations actually increased by 16 percent between 1997 and 1998. In other words, there is an upward

It is probably safe to say that robotisation is still in its initial stages.

trend in Europe and the USA. However, a "revolution" is hardly expected and experts believe more in a continued "evolution".

Automotive industry investment paid off

The automotive industry has been by far the largest user during the entire era of the industrial robot. Volume is a very important element in this field of industry. The investments they have made are now beginning to pay off with interest, particularly in the area of joining, such as welding and gluing, where they are way ahead. The subcontractors to the automotive industry have also learnt to use robot technology to the full and the fact is that the larger system suppliers have in many cases become better than their customers as regards product quality and reliability.

Once the robotics industry realised it was price guiding the automotive industry purchases of production equipment, they introduced standard products for different methods of welding, from spot to laser welding. They also produced standard solutions for dispensing and handling materials, solutions that the automotive industry was not slow to take to. Hydroforming is one example of a new production method introduced in the automotive industry in the nineties. It has lead to a large increase in the number of robots being used for laser cutting.

CHAPTER 10
*A bright future
for the robot*

Removed the dirty work

The success of automation in the automotive industry was also advantageous for the factory workers. The initial fear was that the number of jobs would drastically decrease. Today, we know that the companies who invested in automation are more profitable and expansive, since they produce more. However, the number of employees has not fallen.

Thanks to robot automation, workers have been removed from the dirty, dangerous and monotonous stages of production that existed earlier. Today's operators work in a much better and safer working environment. This has resulted in less sick leave, which has influenced the quality of the products. The improved working environment also makes it easier to recruit to the industry. This will become an important factor for success in the future since the proportion of people between the ages of 25 and 59 will start to drop rapidly after 2015. Indeed, it is estimated that the proportion of people in this active age group in 2050 will be lower in the West than it was in 1950.

Flexible systems

During the 1970s and the early 1980s, the robot manufacturers often had to prove to a sceptical market that automation could offer cost-effective solutions for them. Gradually, the product was accepted in manufacturing but was very limited compared to today's market.

The Aqua Explorer 1000 underwater robot from Japanese KDD was used to inspect the sea bed before laying fibreoptic cables.

In the early days, the market was fragmented into smaller segments and in many cases, especially within the automotive industry, standard products had to make way for more complicated specifications.

The frequent change of models created the need for a system that was more flexible, accessible and of a higher quality. This technological challenge created today's robot industry.

The amount of functions a robot could perform increased in the 1990s. The production lines became more well-balanced and bottlenecks were removed, resulting in better cycle times even for relatively short runs. Meanwhile, the number of robot models increased, which meant that it became easier for customers to find a robot to suit their specific needs.

Not as good at integrating in the USA

In the USA, the automotive industry surpassed all other types of manufacturing industry regarding the ability to take to and invest in automation. At the same time, it can be said that American industry, in comparison with Japanese industry, was not very good at integrating robot technology into its manufacturing. In the USA there are approximately 80,000 industrial robots, while in Japan, with a smaller population and a lower GNP, over 400,000 robots are installed.

On the other hand, the speed with which the Japanese became involved in automation has meant that they invested in equipment when the

CHAPTER 10
*A bright future
for the robot*

prices were at least 30% higher. This means that it will take longer to reach pay off.

With hindsight, it is easy to deduce that the Japanese over-invested in industrial robots. During recent years, the pendulum has started to turn towards Europe and the USA, where the use of robots is increasing while it is decreasing in Japan.

Overcapacity?

The question is, how will the automotive industry develop during the coming decades? Analysts predict an overcapacity of between eight to ten million cars per year in the future.

However, sceptics have predicted this field wrongly before. The automotive industry invests in cycles, since they are very sensitive to the state of the market. The automotive industry has not stopped investing, far from it – it will also be an important customer in the future.

However, it will not only be the automotive industry that invests in industrial robots. Everyday rationalisation in smaller engineering companies may lead to the next important market for robot automation.

The food industry can be just as big

During the 21st century, the food industry will probably become the second largest robot user after the automotive industry. Indeed, some be-

During the 21st century, the food industry will probably become as large a robot user as the automotive industry. The FlexPalletizer is one of the ABB robots that suits the food industry well.

lieve it can become just as big. The food industry, nevertheless, has a turnover that is three times higher than the automotive industry and is becoming increasingly concentrated with fewer, but larger, plants. In this case, the need for automation will increase. Likewise, the demand for quality will be tougher, which also favours robot automation.

The reason that the boom has not yet taken place is that the food industry has not had time to obtain its own expertise, unlike the automotive industry, which has had this proved by its willingness to invest in robots. In addition, the food industry has a lower level of wages than the automotive industry.

The electronics industry is a sector where robot automation of production is growing. In Japan, for example, there are even more robots in the electronics industry than in the automotive industry.

The recognition that painting robots can be good for the industry is increasing steadily. Apart from the environmental aspect, the use of painting robots reduces the consumption of paint. In addition, the most important factor is that the quality of the paintwork is higher than with other methods. The painting of household appliances is an example of another fast

Thanks to their ability to adapt their
working hours to the order situation, robots have become a flexible resource
that can work all hours of the day and
night. Kuka robots working in the automotive industry are shown here.

CHAPTER 10
A bright future for the robot

growing area that opens entirely new markets, where the knowledge gained from painting in the automotive industry can be of use.

Reveal the bottlenecks

Robot automation reveals bottlenecks all around, whether it is the supply of materials or the adjustment of fixtures and tools by workers. When
a robot is installed, greater demands are placed on the fittings working pro-
perly, which will eventually raise the standard of quality.

A robot can do the same thing repeatedly. Therefore, it is not suitable
for spontaneous movements. In this case, humans are far superior. A skilled welder, who should be involved in the programming stage of the robot, can weld just as well as the robot in the short term. However, if you
work the whole week in three shifts, it is difficult for a human to be as alert
all hours of the day.

There are both advantages and disadvantages with robots. One of the
advantages is that they never get tired. They can perform the same task repeatedly and are very precise. The advantage of a human is that they are
able to think and make logical conclusions and thereby adjust the production. In many cases, people are also faster than computers. The motive
for advancing development is now the desire to reduce production costs
for robots, increase their competitiveness compared with human operators and automation, increase the number of operating hours, reduce

operating costs, increase life span and find new applications within all type of industry.

An interdisciplinary enterprise

Construction of industrial robots is an interdisciplinary enterprise. Those who want to devote their time working with the design of robots should be knowledgeable in many different areas, automatic data processing, mathematics, electronics and control techniques for example. The robot manufacturers of today and in the future must produce a robot that is up to the mark when given different tasks. In addition, they must possess a sound knowledge of how servo engineering, electronic engineering and mechanical engineering interact to obtain high precision and speed. It is also important to ascertain how a person best deals with a machine in order to design a workplace that is safe, practical and easy to use.

Guards and vacuum cleaners

Robot manufacturers are also looking for new exciting areas of use outside industry. The robot Spimaster from Cybermotion in Virginia patrolled at random for twelve hours before it went and plugged itself into a socket to recharge. If it suspected a problem, such as an open window or smoke in the air, it would sound the alarm. If an intruder was glimpsed, the robot filmed him.

In the USA, there are mass-produced home robots that do the vacuum cleaning; the robot is controlled by a home computer. The home is first mapped into the computer so that the robot knows where to go. Then, the owner programs the robot to do certain things at different times, such as fetching the mail, vacuum cleaning or carrying the dishes in and out. In addition, Electrolux in Sweden has produced an automatic vacuum cleaner.

Another area in which robots are advancing is sorting mail. Among oth-

The Help Mate service robot is used in the field of health care to assist nurses.

ers, the US Postal Service and ABB have initiated a collaborative effort in this field.

Service robots are on the march

Service robots have become a group to be reckoned with. For instance, "The father of robotics", Joseph Engelberger, has become involved via his company Help Mate. They have developed a robot that is used in the medical services to assist nurses. Development is also being carried out to launch a robot for elderly care. This robot will be able to speak to the elderly, cook food, go for walks with them and take their blood pressure, for example. Joseph Engelberger hopes to be able to reduce productions costs for the service robots to such a level that the elderly can afford to hire a robot for a just a few dollars a day.

The future of service robots is still an unknown quantity but the industrial robot has become an important aid in industry that has saved many worn out backs and lost money. Therefore, it is appropriate that we now, on the eve of a new century, raise our glasses and toast the industrial robot – the extended arm of man being manufactured by around ten companies operating in the global market.

CHAPTER 10
*A bright future
for the robot*

More and more robots are being used in the food industry. Here, three IRB 6400 robots are handling milk crates at MD Foods in Tystrup, Denmark.

A FEW ROBOT STATISTICS Source: *World Robotics* 1999

In 1998, the latest year for which statistics are available, there were approximately 71,000 industrial robots installed in the world compared with 85,000 the year before. The ECE (Economic Commission for Europe) and IFR calculate that approximately 97,000 robots will be installed in the year 2002. In 1998, there were a total of 720,000 robots already installed world-wide. This figure is calculated to rise to 800,000 in 2002.

New robot installations 1998

1.	Japan	34,000
2.	USA	11,000
3.	Germany	10,000
4.	Italy	4,000
5.	Spain	2,000
6.	France	2,000

Total number of installed industrial robots

1.	Japan	412,000
2.	USA	82,000
3.	Germany	73,000
4.	Italy	32,000
5.	South Korea	31,000
6.	France	16,000

Number of industrial robots per 10,000 people employed in industry

1.	Japan	279
2.	Singapore	140
3.	South Korea	104
4.	Germany	100
5.	Italy	70
6.	Sweden	66

Printed sources

A Competitive Assessment of the US (1985), US Department of Commerce.

Ayres, R & Miller, S (1982), *Robotics Applications and Social Implications,* Ballinger, Cambridge.

Christopher Polhem Minnesskrift (1911), Svenska Teknologföreningen, Stockholm.

Eco, U & Zorzoli, G (1961), *Uppfinningarnas historia,* Natur och Kultur, Stockholm.

Engelberger, J (1980), *Robotics in practice,* Kogan Page, Amersham.

Engelberger, J (1989), *Robotics in service,* Kogan Page, London.

Gould, W (1996), *Business in action Ford, Cherytree Books,* Bath.

Gray J O and Caldwell D G, (1996), *Advanced Robotics & Intelligent machines,* The Institution of Electrical Engineers, Herts.

Industrirobotar i gjuterier, (1974), IVF, Gothenburg.

Industrirobotar i Europa (1993), Utlandsrapport från Sveriges Tekniska Attachéer.

Industrirobotar i Japan (1981), Utlandsrapport från Sveriges Tekniska Attachéer.

Industrirobotar i Japan (1990), Utlandsrapport från Sveriges Tekniska Attachéer.

Industrirobotar i Japan (1995), Utlandsrapport från Sveriges Tekniska Attachéer.

Industrirobotar krav och villkor vid användning, (1975), IVF, Gothenburg.

Industrirobotar i Sovjet (1981), Utlandsrapport från Sveriges Tekniska Attachéer.

Industrirobotar i Västtyskland (1984), Utlandsrapport från Sveriges Tekniska Attachéer

Lindroth, S (1951), *Christopher Polhem och Stora Kopparberget,* Stora Kopparbergs Bergslags Aktiebolag.

Lund, J (1988), *Från kula till data,* Gidlunds.

Martins, JB and Svensson M (1988), *Profitability and industrial robots,* IFS.

Nof, S (1985), *Handbook of Industrial Robotics,* (John Wiley & Sons), New York.

Strandh, S (1985), *Polhem – mekanikens mästare,* Natur och Kultur, Stockholm.

13th International Symposium on Industrial Robots Conference Proceedings (1983), RI

World Robotics 1998, IFR and UN.

World Robotics 1999, IFR and UN.

Wrege, C & Greenwood, R (1991). *Frederick W. Taylor The Father of Scientific Management,* Irwin, New York.

ABB Robotics press archive.

Brochures, websites and annual reports from various robot manufacturers.

Oral sources

Anders Arnström, KTH
Percy Barnevik, ABB
Gunnar Bolmsjö, Lund University
Håkan Brantmark, ABB
Christina Bredin, ABB
Erik Casserdahl, previously Svenska Metallverken
Hans Collén, ABB
Gunnar Christenssen, previously Atlas Copco
Stelio Demark, previously ABB
Håkan Emilsson, HE Maskinservice
Joseph Engelberger, Help Mate, previously Unimation
Nils-Gunnar Fenander, ABB
Kenneth Håkansson, previously Kockums
Bo Indebetou, previously Atlas Copco
Jan Jonsson, ABB
Jan Karlsson, UN
Ove Kullborg, ABB
Ted Lindbom, previously Unimation
Åke Lindqvist, ABB
Åke Madesäter, ABB
Gösta Martins, previously ABB
Nils Mårtensson, Chalmers University of Technology
Ulf-Göran Norefors, ABB
Lars Erik Ringström, ABB
Sven Sjöqvist, ABB
Hans Skoog, ABB
Göran Stensson, ABB
Felix Sundkvist, Comau
Björn Weichbrodt, VI, previously ABB

A toast with champagne for the industrial robot is very appropriate, as a large number of today's champagne producers use robots in their processes.